Conflict Resolution for Kids

Simple Strategies to Help Children Resolve Disagreements, Develop Problem-Solving Skills, and Foster Positive Relationships

Table of Contents

Introduction

Have you ever noticed that children argue and fight a lot, a lot more than adults? They seem to be in a never-ending tug-of-war over toys, treats, and everything in between. Maybe the following scene is familiar: your living room transforms into a battlefield as your children clash over the remote control, each determined to watch their favorite show. Perhaps the seemingly endless dispute about who gets the last cookie leaves you bewildered and wondering if you're the referee in a never-ending wrestling match. It's a familiar scenario, isn't it? As parents, you might often find yourself caught in the whirlwind of your children's conflicts, witnessing trivial arguments evolve into something overwhelmingly frequent and intense.

While it's tempting to swoop in and resolve every dispute, you know deep down that you can't shield your children from all the challenges they'll face as they navigate the complexities of life. As much as you'd like to be their constant protectors, you must recognize that they need more than just a safety net – they need the skills to manage disagreements and conflicts independently.

Just like adults, children experience a wide range of emotions and desires. From their frustration when their playmate grabs a cherished toy to the ongoing rivalry between siblings over who gets the bigger slice of cake, these everyday scenarios hold the seeds of growth and learning within them. What might appear as minor squabbles can actually serve as important building blocks for their emotional development.

When you teach your children effective conflict-resolution skills from an early age, you provide them with tools that will serve them well throughout their lives. Imagine the impact of a child who can confidently express their needs and boundaries and communicate with others to find common ground and navigate the rough waters of disagreement without resorting to tantrums or tears. These skills are not just about avoiding fights; they are about empowering your children to stand up for themselves while respecting the needs and feelings of others.

Conflict resolution isn't just about finding solutions to arguments. It's a profound way of developing emotional intelligence. When children learn to understand their own feelings and the feelings of those around them, they gain a deeper understanding of the human experience. This emotional awareness becomes an invaluable tool, guiding them through the challenges of school, friendships, and, eventually, the adult world.

In the following chapters, we've included numerous activities and exercises that will teach your children conflict resolution. You will explore practical strategies and engaging activities that will help your child become adept at resolving disagreements healthily and constructively. As a parent, you have the chance to lay the foundation for a future generation that can communicate effectively, collaborate peacefully, and approach conflicts with empathy and understanding.

Chapter 1: The Cause and Course of Conflict

Even though no one likes to deal with them, conflicts, disagreements, and arguments are a part of life. When people have different opinions, desires, needs, or goals, it can lead to disagreements during conversations. However, if the disagreements are expressed in a verbally aggressive manner, they turn into conflicts. A serious disagreement arises when people have opposing actions, motives, needs, values, goals, and obligations.

While it's easier for adults to tackle the surge of emotions after a conflict, adequate guidance and training are crucial for conflict resolution for children. They are simply not equipped to tackle these feelings. Therefore, primary caregivers must work with children to navigate conflicts healthily and constructively.

When people have different opinions, desires, needs, or goals, it can lead to disagreements during conversations.
https://pixabay.com/photos/cute-couple-love-misunderstanding-5392897/

The Causes of Conflict in Children

Group Dynamics: Children often form groups when playing or socializing. Conflicts can arise when there's disagreement about who's in charge, how decisions are made, or if someone feels excluded.

Desire for Independence: Children seek more control over their choices as they grow. Conflicts can occur when they want to do things their way, resist following adult instructions, or assert their autonomy.

Peer Influence: Children value fitting in with their peers. Conflicts can happen when they feel pressured to conform to their friends' preferences or behaviors, even if it goes against their wishes.

Personal Belongings: Disputes over personal belongings can lead to conflicts. Borrowing things without permission, not returning borrowed items, or accidentally damaging belongings can cause disagreements.

Lack of Empathy: Children are still learning to understand others' feelings. Conflicts can arise when they unintentionally hurt someone's feelings, leading to misunderstandings and hurt emotions.

Unstructured Play: During unstructured play, children may have different ideas about how to play. Conflicts can occur when they can't agree on the game's direction or how to include everyone.

Competition for Attention: Children seek attention from adults and peers. Conflicts can arise when they feel overshadowed or left out, leading to disagreements over who deserves recognition.

Language Barriers: In various settings, language differences can hinder communication and lead to misunderstandings. Children might struggle to express themselves or understand their peers, causing conflicts.

Stereotyping and Prejudice: Conflicts can stem from biases children encounter based on characteristics like gender, race, or background. Stereotypes and prejudice can lead to hurt feelings and misunderstandings.

Physical Space: Sharing spaces can lead to conflicts over personal boundaries, organization, and resource use. Disagreements can arise when children have differing ideas about how to use the space.

Unmet Expectations: Conflicts can occur when children's expectations don't match reality. They might have imagined a different outcome for an activity or event, leading to frustration.

Social Hierarchy: Children may establish informal hierarchies within peer groups. Conflicts can arise over who's in charge or who is more popular within the group.

Comparisons: Children might feel pressured when they get compared to siblings or peers. Conflicts can arise due to the stress of having to meet perceived expectations or prove themselves.

Cultural Differences: Conflicts can emerge from misunderstandings about cultural norms and practices. Children from different backgrounds may interact differently, leading to conflicts or clashes.

Fear and Insecurity: Children might experience conflicts due to underlying fears or insecurities. New experiences or changes can trigger emotional responses, leading to disagreements.

Children may experience conflicts due to fear.

Understanding these nuanced causes of conflicts can help adults provide targeted guidance and interventions to support children in resolving disputes, building strong social skills, and developing effective conflict-resolution strategies.

The Progression of Conflict

The progression of conflict in children commonly follows some typical stages. Understanding these stages can help parents and caregivers better support children as they learn to navigate and resolve conflicts. Here's an overview of how conflict tends to evolve in children:

Initial Disagreement: Conflict often begins with a simple disagreement. This can be about sharing toys, choosing an activity, or any situation where children have differing opinions or desires. Imagine two friends, Sarah and Emily, playing together. They both want to play with a favorite toy, but there's only one available. This initial disagreement is a common scenario among children.

Expression of Feelings: Children may express their feelings more intensely as the conflict escalates. This can include frustration, anger, sadness, or even confusion. They might use words, gestures, or facial expressions to convey emotions. Sarah expresses her frustration, saying, "I wanted to play with that first! It's not fair." Emily responds defensively, "Well, I saw it first, and I want to play with it too." Both children express their feelings, but the tension begins to rise.

Escalation: If the disagreement is not resolved, the conflict can escalate. Children might raise their voices, use more intense body language, or even resort to name-calling. This stage can sometimes involve more emotional outbursts. As the disagreement continues, it becomes more heated. Sarah raises her voice, saying, "You always take what you want!" Emily retorts, "That's not true, you're just being selfish!" The conflict is escalating as they exchange accusations.

Physical Actions: In some cases, conflicts can become physical and involve pushing, hitting, or grabbing. This needs to be addressed as quickly as possible. If the disagreement remains unresolved, it could escalate further. In this case, Sarah might snatch the toy from Emily's hands, and Emily might angrily push her away.

Seeking Adult Help: Children often turn to adults, such as parents, caregivers, or teachers, when conflicts become overwhelming or they struggle to resolve them independently. Seeking help from trusted adults is a positive step, showing that children recognize their limits and seek guidance. At this point, a caregiver or teacher might step in to address the situation. They separate the children and ask them to explain what happened. Both children explain their perspectives but are still upset and unwilling to compromise.

Negotiation and Resolution: With adult guidance, one can learn negotiation skills and conflict resolution strategies. This might involve teaching them to take turns, share, compromise, and find win-win solutions that meet the needs of everyone involved. With adult guidance, the children begin to negotiate a solution. The caregiver suggests they take turns playing with the toy or find another activity they both enjoy. After some discussion, they agree to take turns and eventually settle down to play together.

Understanding and Empathy: Children can develop a deeper understanding of others' perspectives and emotions. They might learn to empathize with their peers and consider how their actions impact others.

Communication Skills: As children mature, they can develop better communication skills, which allow them to express their thoughts and feelings more effectively and listen actively to others.

Conflict Prevention: With experience and guidance, children can also learn strategies to prevent conflicts from escalating. They might practice effective communication, problem-solving, and self-regulation to address disagreements before they become major issues.

Conflict Resolution Independence: Children become more capable of resolving conflicts independently as they grow. They learn from their experiences and apply their newfound skills to navigate disagreements with increasing confidence.

Real-Life Example: Sibling Rivalry

Imagine two siblings, Alex and Jamie, arguing over who chooses the TV show. Alex wants to watch a cartoon, while Jamie wants to watch a documentary.

As the argument progresses, Alex starts calling Jamie's choice boring, and Jamie responds by making fun of Alex's favorite cartoon. The disagreement escalates to shouting and name-calling.

Without intervention, the conflict could escalate. Alex might forcefully change the TV channel, and Jamie might retaliate by blocking the remote. This could lead to a physical scuffle.

A parent steps in, separates the siblings, and discusses finding a compromise. Eventually, they agree to watch one cartoon episode and then switch to the documentary.

Minor disagreements among children can quickly escalate if not properly addressed. By recognizing the stages of conflict progression and intervening with effective communication, active listening, and negotiation skills, adults can guide children toward resolving conflicts in healthy and constructive ways. This helps children learn valuable life skills and fosters positive relationships. Just as in the real-life example of sibling rivalry, parents can play a crucial role in de-escalating conflicts and promoting resolution. It is essential for parents and caregivers to be aware of these stages and to intervene appropriately when conflicts arise. Providing guidance, teaching conflict resolution skills, and modeling healthy communication can help children develop the tools to handle conflicts positively and constructively.

The Effects of Unresolved Conflicts

Unresolved conflicts can significantly impact children's emotional health and social interactions. When conflicts are not properly addressed or resolved, they can negatively affect a child's well-being and relationships. Here's how unresolved conflicts can impact children.

Emotional Distress: Unresolved conflicts can trigger a range of intense emotions in children. For example, suppose a child constantly argues with a friend over the rules of a game. In that case, they might feel frustrated because their perspective isn't being acknowledged. Over time, this consistent emotional distress can contribute to a negative emotional state, affecting the child's overall happiness and mental well-being.

Low Self-Esteem: When conflicts persist, children may internalize the idea that they are incapable of solving problems or achieving positive outcomes. For instance, if a child's opinions are repeatedly dismissed during disagreements, they might start doubting their own judgment. This can lead to a decreased sense of self-worth and a lack of confidence in their abilities.

Relationship Strain: Unresolved conflicts can strain relationships between children, siblings, or peers. For instance, if two siblings constantly argue about sharing responsibilities at home, their relationship might become strained. This strain can manifest as increased tension, reduced communication, and a lack of trust, making it difficult for them to collaborate and maintain healthy relationships.

Communication Issues: When conflicts are not properly resolved, children miss out on valuable opportunities to develop effective communication skills. For example, suppose two classmates have an ongoing disagreement about a group project. In that case, they may need to learn how to express their concerns clearly, listen actively, or find common ground. This lack of skill development can hinder their ability to communicate effectively in various contexts, affecting both personal and professional interactions later in life.

Aggressive Behavior: Children who experience unresolved conflicts might resort to aggressive behavior as a way to cope with their emotions. For instance, a child frustrated by constant disagreements with a peer might start yelling or using hurtful language. This aggressive behavior can create a cycle where conflicts escalate further, potentially harming relationships and emotional well-being.

Avoidance Behavior: In response to unresolved conflicts, children might develop avoidance behaviors to sidestep situations that could lead to disagreements. For instance, a child with an ongoing conflict with a playmate might start avoiding that playmate altogether to prevent conflicts. Over time, this avoidance behavior can limit the child's social interactions and opportunities for growth.

Impact on Learning: Persistent conflicts can divert a child's attention from important tasks such as schoolwork. For example, a child preoccupied with a conflict involving a classmate might struggle to focus during lessons or complete assignments. This can hurt their academic performance and hinder their overall learning experience.

Long-Term Effects: If children don't learn effective conflict resolution skills early on, they might carry the resulting unresolved issues into adolescence and adulthood. For example, a child who never learns how to navigate conflicts with empathy and understanding might struggle to form and maintain healthy relationships later in life. These unresolved conflicts can contribute to a cycle of negative interactions that affect various aspects of their well-being.

Negative Modeling: Children learn by observing the behavior of adults and peers around them. If they witness unresolved conflicts between adults, such as parents or caregivers, they may internalize the belief that conflicts are unsolvable. For instance, if a child observes their parents constantly arguing without reaching resolutions, they may replicate this pattern in their interactions, perpetuating unhealthy conflict dynamics.

Emotional Suppression: In an attempt to avoid conflicts, children might suppress their emotions. For example, if a child experiences ongoing disagreements with a friend, they might choose to suppress their feelings of frustration to maintain the relationship. However, suppressing emotions can lead to emotional problems later in life as these unresolved feelings accumulate, potentially resulting in anxiety or depression.

Reduced Empathy: Unresolved conflicts can hinder the development of empathy, a crucial social and emotional skill. For instance, if a child repeatedly clashes with a peer over different opinions, they might struggle to understand the peer's perspective or feelings. This can hinder the child's ability to connect with others on an emotional level, impacting their social interactions and relationships.

Academic and Social Performance: The emotional burden of unresolved conflicts can spill over into various aspects of a child's life. For example, ongoing conflicts with classmates might distract a child during group activities, negatively impacting their contribution and overall performance. Similarly, unresolved conflicts can affect a child's ability to engage in cooperative play or teamwork, hindering their social development and ability to collaborate effectively with others.

In essence, unresolved conflicts can have profound and multifaceted impacts on children's emotional health and social interactions. Recognizing and addressing these impacts through effective conflict resolution strategies, open communication, and emotional support is vital for promoting children's well-being and helping them develop healthy relationships as they grow and navigate the complexities of social life.

Conflict Resolution Strategies

Implementing strategies to help children manage and resolve conflicts is crucial for their holistic development and well-being. These strategies equip children with essential skills beyond conflict resolution, fostering emotional intelligence, effective communication, and future success. By teaching children to identify triggers, they gain self-awareness and recognize patterns in their emotional responses. Moreover, imparting self-regulation skills empowers children to manage their emotions during conflicts through techniques like deep breathing and positive self-talk. Constructive feedback strategies guide children in expressing their feelings respectfully using "I" statements, fostering empathy and understanding.

These strategies play a pivotal role in nurturing crucial life skills. They facilitate emotional regulation, enabling children to cope with stress and enhance self-esteem. Effective communication skills acquired through conflict resolution strategies are fundamental for building healthy relationships and achieving success in various life domains. Problem-solving abilities honed during conflict resolution empower children to tackle challenges with confidence. Furthermore, these strategies cultivate empathy, laying the groundwork for positive connections and collaboration. Implementing these conflict resolution strategies in children's lives ensures their emotional well-being, reduces stress, and promotes a positive outlook, setting the stage for a fulfilling and successful future.

Identifying Triggers

Encouraging parents to help their children identify triggers involves engaging in open and reflective conversations. Parents can ask specific questions like, "Can you think of a time when you felt upset during a disagreement?" This prompts children to recall past conflicts and consider the factors that led to their emotional responses. These conversations foster self-awareness and help children recognize patterns in their emotions.

Role-play scenarios provide a hands-on approach to understanding triggers. Parents can act out different conflict situations with their children, demonstrating various triggers and emotional reactions. This interactive method helps children connect emotions to specific situations, making it easier for them to identify triggers in real-life conflicts.

Self-Regulation Skills

Teaching children self-regulation skills involves providing practical techniques to manage their emotions during conflicts. Parents can explain deep breathing exercises as a way to calm down. For instance, they might guide their child to take slow, deep breaths while counting to four for each inhale and exhale. This simple technique helps children manage their physiological responses to stress and anxiety.

Counting to ten before responding is another self-regulation strategy. Parents can emphasize the importance of briefly pausing to collect thoughts before reacting emotionally. This empowers children to approach conflicts with a clearer mind, allowing for more thoughtful and measured responses.

Encouraging positive self-talk is essential for building emotional resilience. Parents can teach children to reframe negative thoughts into positive ones. For example, if a child is feeling frustrated during a conflict, they can remind themselves that they have the ability to handle the situation calmly and find a solution.

Constructive Feedback

Guiding children to provide and receive feedback constructively involves teaching them effective communication skills. Parents can explain the concept of "I" statements, where individuals express their feelings without blaming others. For example, instead of saying, "You never listen to me," a child can say, "I feel unheard when we don't discuss things together."

Role-playing scenarios come into play again when practicing "I" statements. Parents can act as peers in conflict scenarios, encouraging the child to express their thoughts and emotions using this constructive approach. This practice helps children feel more confident using "I" statements in real-life conflicts.

Through these strategies, parents can empower their children by:

Creating a Conflict Resolution Toolkit: Parents and children can work together to create a physical or mental toolkit that includes a list of identified triggers, self-regulation techniques, and examples of "I" statements. This toolkit serves as a personalized guide for handling conflicts.

Modeling Conflict Resolution: Parents demonstrate healthy conflict resolution by openly discussing and resolving disagreements with each other. Children observe this positive behavior and learn that conflicts can be addressed both calmly and constructively.

Encouraging Open Dialogue: Parents create an environment where children feel comfortable sharing their experiences and emotions by regularly checking in with them about their conflicts. Open communication ensures that parents can provide guidance and support as needed.

Reinforcing Positive Efforts: When children successfully apply these conflict resolution strategies, parents should acknowledge and praise their efforts. Positive reinforcement encourages children to continue using these skills and boosts their self-confidence.

Applying Skills Beyond Conflicts: Parents should highlight that the skills learned in conflict resolution have broader applications. From group projects at school to interactions with friends and family, these skills contribute to improved social interactions and emotional intelligence.

By implementing these strategies and providing ongoing guidance, parents play a crucial role in equipping their children with the tools and confidence needed to navigate conflicts effectively. As children internalize these skills, they develop into more resilient, empathetic, and capable individuals who can positively approach conflicts.

Chapter 2: The Language of Emotion

You must be familiar with expressions like "Emotions were running high," "We were in the heat of the moment," and "I lost my head, and everything went to hell." All of these statements have something in common. You guessed it, Emotions! Emotions are a primary contributor to diffusing or heightening any conflict. The methods by which people convey their emotions to each other and communicate their feelings can easily make or break a relationship. Often, when people describe themselves as hot-headed or emotional, the brain is conditioned to believe these labels. It sends out signals and triggers thoughts to confirm those beliefs. This process tends to make it harder to learn how to efficiently use constructive emotional language since you're already working overtime to dismantle the old image you have of yourself.

It's quite common in stressful situations for strong emotions, like anger and fear, to bubble up to the surface or simmer right below it. Choosing the correct language to express yourself in these situations takes practice and requires much self-regulation and control.

Emotions are a primary contributor to diffusing or heightening any conflict.

Now, imagine what it would be like for a child who's still trying to make their way in the world and understand the labeling of every emotion they experience. Children aren't born with a natural ability to control and communicate their feelings. They learn how to gain control by following their parents' example, so always assume you're being watched. Most children model their reactions and emotional responses based on the environment that they live in and how their caregivers respond to them.

In many cases, parents assume that this is their cue to display the perfect example of emotional intelligence, which usually entails pushing down emotions and responses to feign control. To an outsider, that seems like the perfect scenario. However, children learn more when you show them the learning process. Acknowledging that you are not perfect and not always fluent in the language of emotions gives them the push they need to accept that as long as you learn from them, it's okay to make mistakes. Being emotional in front of your children doesn't show you in a weak light. It just tells them you're human like them and shows an example of someone actively working to better themselves.

What Is the Language of Emotions?

Your emotions and sensations are given meaning and value through the language you use to express them. In many situations, the words you use to describe how you feel can accentuate the feelings, be it positive or negative. As you give names to your feelings, you may find that this has a psychological and physical effect. In the 1700s, the emotions linked to "homesickness" were quickly referred to as a fatal condition afflicting the masses. The yearning people felt for their homes distressed them enough to display symptoms of exhaustion, running fevers, and overall desolation. People started developing eating disorders and eventually withering away. In this day and age, the general population does not perceive homesickness in the same light. Therefore, the perception of the words and the feelings associated with them have changed.

If that example teaches you anything, it is to put the overall picture into perspective. Do not dramatize or undermine emotions, but give them their fair amount of recognition. Using big words to describe small actions or giving a strong emotional reaction in a sensitive situation can disturb the balance and connection you have with your children. Most importantly, before you start teaching your children the right way to express themselves, you must make sure you understand it yourself first. Think of it as a journey you're embarking on together in one small boat, and the emotional conflicts you face are the waves you have to go over to reach the mainland.

Understanding and Managing Emotions

As your child ventures through the land of emotions, they will require as much guidance as you can provide to navigate it properly. If done correctly, young children and adolescents who can successfully and effectively express their emotions are better at controlling their impulses. They also take less time to overcome hard feelings like anger and disappointment. The more they are able to regulate their feelings, the healthier their relationships will be, whether it's with you, the rest of the family, or with the friends they make along the way.

With your help, they will learn to identify and give names to their feelings. This is the first step in teaching control and emotional intelligence. The guidance you provide will differ significantly depending on which age group your child is in.

Talk about It

With younger children, the probability of emotions suddenly running high is more common than you think. Young children tend to experience a lot of emotions they can't name. You can explain scenes unfolding before you, for instance, a child crying as their parents leave the park. You can ask your child to guess the emotion and take note of the facial expressions and body language. This helps them pick up non-verbal cues to different emotions.

Also, make sure you're labeling the emotions correctly, "they're crying, they must be sad to leave," "you're smiling, you must be happy."

Use Stories

You can explore emotions through picture books.
https://unsplash.com/photos/qtUAV-_yWZc?utm_source=unsplash&utm_medium=referral&utm_content=creditShareLink

Explore emotions in stories and picture books. Talk with them about the different characters and how various emotions are displayed in the illustrations. Make a list of emotional vocabulary, and see if they can reenact the emotion to you later on.

Ensure they understand that each person has their own mental castle of emotions. Explain that emotions can be hidden. Have them understand that just because they don't show it on their face, it doesn't mean they don't feel it. Give examples of your own mental universe to get them to share theirs.

Model Your Emotions to Them

"I was so mad when I broke that glass that I yelled afterward. Do you do that when you feel angry?". Showing your child how to label and recognize your own emotions teaches them to name theirs. Explain how this may affect them physically, "You look worried; does your tummy feel funny."

Teach Simple Coping Strategies

With younger children, you can start by teaching them basic calming techniques, such as taking a deep breath a few times in a row or counting to 20 in their heads when they feel overwhelmed.

You can also give examples of physical action to deal with stronger emotions, like jumping up and down and clapping when excited or asking for a hug when upset.

Adapt Your Strategy to Their Age

Most of the previous tips work wonderfully with younger children still exploring the spectrum of emotions, but what about older ones, teens, and preteens?

If you have a child entering that phase, you're in for a ride on an emotional roller coaster. Children within this age group acutely feel strong emotions, like anger, humiliation, and shame. They probably have the vocabulary to know the meaning of these emotions. However, they may not necessarily know how to recognize them within themselves.

- If you sense emotions rising, step in. The earlier the child can identify the point when they experience emotional changes, the easier it will be to stay in control.
- As with younger children, point out the physical impact of strong emotions. "Yesterday, when I was stuck in traffic, I was so upset that my heart started racing, and I was sweating. Does that ever happen to you?".
- Point out outward behaviors to emotions, like hitting the keys on the keyboard too hard or pressing too hard on a pen when writing. Ask them if they need a minute to get some air and calm down.
- Explore coping mechanisms you use to calm yourself. "When I feel low and displaced with myself, I try to focus on the things I've done that make me proud."
- Give other examples of how to deal with strong emotions and release pent-up energy. Try going for a run, breathwork, meditation, dancing, reading, drawing, or even listening to loud music. Try to tailor the options to things your child will enjoy doing.

Red Flags of Emotional Struggle

Different children have different coping mechanisms for strong emotions.

- You may notice your child responding inappropriately to bad news, like laughing.
- They switch between emotions really fast, from calm to angry to stoic.
- They may try to hide their emotions and push people away when overwhelmed.
- They struggle with letting go of things that upset them long after the situation ends.
- They can't relax enough to enjoy their time with loved ones or while doing things they enjoy.

Exercises to Improve Resilience and the Use of Language to Express Emotions

There are a ton of resources on navigating conflicting emotions and how to control and regulate your inner turmoil. Now, all you need to do is tailor said exercises to be more child-friendly and fun to engage in.

Name It and Tame It

How Do You Feel Today?

happy   angry   nervous   jealous

confused   shy   disgusted   scared

cry   loving   tired   disappointed

If you've never heard of the "How are you feeling today" charts or flashcards, you're in for a treat. This exercise is more suitable for younger children, ages 4 and 5. There are versions of the chart for older children, with more complex emotional vocabulary included to help them express emotions more efficiently.

These charts are often used more than once a day to identify the feelings your child is dealing with. They include illustrations of different emotions, complete with the name of the emotion below it.

Ask your child to point to the emotion they're feeling each time, and follow suit to emphasize that you're in this together. Don't stop at one emotion; encourage them to choose more than one picture. Ensure they understand that having mixed feelings is common and that it's normal to have more than one emotion.

As they continue to pick different emotions, they'll become more articulate in expressing themselves, especially if they're with their siblings of different ages.

Be sure to emphasize that even though we cannot always control how we feel, we can control our responses.

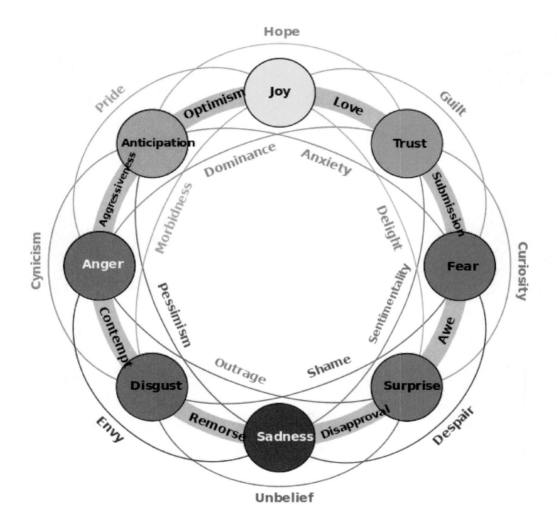

Ensure they understand that having mixed feelings is common and that it's normal to have more than one emotion.
ChaoticBrain, CC BY-SA 4.0 <https://creativecommons.org/licenses/by-sa/4.0>, via Wikimedia Commons: https://commons.wikimedia.org/wiki/File:Plutchik_Dyads.svg

Roll the Dice

The numbers on the dice can represent taste, smell, and more.
https://www.pexels.com/photo/photo-of-two-red-dices-965879/

Make a list of different adjectives that describe your child and every family member, and encourage your child to do the same. These words can be negative or positive, like mean, kind, lovely, or dumb. Write each word on a piece of paper and turn it over.

The numbers on the dice represent the following;

- 1 is taste
- 2 is smell
- 3 is texture
- 4 is color
- 5 is weight
- 6 is shape

Ask one of the family members to turn over a sheet of paper and roll the dice. If, for instance, they roll a 2, and the word on the sheet is dumb, what does it smell like when someone calls you dumb? The answers you tend to get from these questions will differ according to age. Younger children may say something like, "It smells like doo-doo when someone calls me dumb." Older children may be more articulate. For instance, if they roll a 5 and have the word kind, they may say it feels like the weight of 1,000 pounds as they feel the obligation to be kind again.

Besides working on their creativity, this game gives them a new way to express themselves. You can add another dice and include brightness, sounds, or temperature to the game as they get better at it.

Write It Down

Journaling is a powerful tool to introduce to your children to help them with their emotional expression. Sometimes, the only way to figure out how you truly feel is to put pen to paper and write the first things that come to mind. People are often surprised by what comes out on the paper when they're not overly fixated on their emotions.

Give your child the choice between keeping their journals to themselves or allowing you to read them at the end of the day.

Chapter 3: The Art of Active Listening

Contrary to what many people think, good listening skills don't come naturally to children. Although it might seem like something basic, children often struggle with actively listening and paying attention to a conversation because they're usually distracted and overstimulated. With all the gadgets and technology clamoring for their attention, it's no surprise that children sometimes struggle to focus on conversations. This can often lead to misunderstandings and conflict. For instance, maybe you're talking to your child about weekend plans, but they're so fixated on their favorite toy that your words seem to vanish into thin air. It's like you're speaking a different language, and you can't help but say, "I just want you to listen." What you don't understand is that your child doesn't know how to behave otherwise. If they have never been taught active listening skills, their communication skills will always suffer, and conflicts will be even more difficult to manage. Active listening isn't just about "listening." It involves giving your full attention to the speaker and trying your best to understand and interpret what the other person is trying to convey. Both verbal and nonverbal listening cues are used in active listening.

Active listening isn't just about "listening."

Why Active Listening Is Important

Teaching your child to be an active listener comes with a bunch of rewards! Not only will they perform well academically, but they will also become great at making friends and finding solutions to problems. Also, being a good listener shows they have a heart of gold and are totally committed. If you're hoping they'll be leaders in the future, active listening will be their stepping stone. Some benefits of active listening include:

- Increased productivity
- Enhanced self-reliance
- Quicker work pace
- Boosted resourcefulness
- Fewer misunderstandings

Active Listening vs. Passive Listening

Have you ever tried chatting with your child and felt like their attention was elsewhere? That's passive listening – they hear the words, but nothing is registering. When they're like this, the information just goes in one ear and out the other. Active listening is the better alternative. In order to actively listen, one must comprehend the argument the other is attempting to make rather than just hearing it.

Five Steps of Active Listening

You can show your children the ropes of active listening by being an active listener yourself. When you demonstrate this, they can understand how valuable it is. Improve both your and your child's active listening game with these 5 tips:

- **Maintain Eye Contact**

Maintaining eye contact gives an impression of being trustworthy, friendly, sociable, honest, confident, and attentive. Concentrating on the eyes can boost your focus, helping you grasp the speaker's words more completely.

- **Don't Interrupt**

Give the speaker the space to finish their thought before you jump in with your response. Avoid interrupting, finishing their sentences, or rushing them. Don't try to guess or assume where their thoughts are headed—doing so can hinder effective communication.

- **Ask Questions**

One effective way to demonstrate your attentive listening and ensure accurate understanding is by asking targeted questions about what's being shared. This not only helps clear up any uncertainties but also shows your genuine interest. Here are four types of questions you can try:

  o **Open-Ended:** These encourage more detailed discussions.

    For example: "Can you tell me more about your day at school?"

  o **Close-Ended:** These seek specific answers.

    For example: "Have you completed your homework?"

- **Leading:** These guide the response in a certain direction.

  For example: "Do you find that you have too much homework?"

- **Reflective:** These prompt deeper insights.

  For example: "You mentioned that math is your favorite subject; what makes it so interesting for you?"

Using these types of questions helps build a stronger connection and emphasizes your genuine commitment to understanding the speaker's viewpoint.

- **Repeat Back What the Speaker Says**

A helpful way to ensure that you've grasped the speaker's message is to rephrase it using your own words. This confirms your understanding and lets you capture the main points. By summarizing the key elements, you show active involvement and allow the speaker to correct any misunderstandings.

- **Listen for Total Meaning**

When someone communicates, there are two main aspects to consider: what they're saying (the content) and the emotions or attitudes accompanying it. Both these elements hold importance and add depth to the message. So, when you're listening, it's essential to focus on both the actual words and the underlying feelings. At times, rather than just the textual information, the message's true meaning is better grasped through the emotions transmitted.

By implementing these suggestions, you and your child will quickly acquire the fundamental abilities required to become better active listeners. Using these strategies together, you can help your child develop better listening skills.

Active Listening Activities

Teaching your child how to be an active listener by leading by example is just the beginning. To truly develop and enhance these skills, hands-on practice is key. Here are some enjoyable activities to assist in nurturing and refining your child's listening abilities:

- **Story Time:** Encourage your child to make predictions as you read them stories. They are encouraged to pay close attention to the details during this exercise, which will help them develop rational guesses.

Your child can make predictions about a story when you're reading it together.

- **Act Out the Story:** Take turns acting out different parts with your child after reading a story. Let them predict and imagine how characters might react next. This not only engages their listening skills but also encourages creative thinking.
- **Cook Together:** Involve your child in the cooking process. Read the recipe aloud and have them follow each step precisely.
- **Share Interests:** Engage in conversations about subjects that intrigue your child. Because of this, they get a chance to practice speaking and listening in actual discussions.
- **Telephone Game:** Get a few people involved to make this game fun. Whisper a sentence from one person to another, passing it along until it reaches the final person. Compare the original sentence with the final version to see how it changed.
- **Question Exchange:** Collaborate with your child to create a list of questions for them to ask you or a sibling. After answering, challenge each other to recall as many answers as possible, then switch roles and assess the other person's performance.
- **Spot the Change:** Play the "spot the change" game by reading a short story to your child, then rereading it with alterations. Encourage them to clap or raise their hand whenever they notice a change.
- **Follow Directions:** Provide brief, simple instructions and have your child follow them to create drawings based on what they hear.

Developing improved listening skills demands dedication and focus. By engaging in active listening exercises, children can enhance their communication abilities and cultivate a valuable skill set for life.

Developing improved listening skills demands dedication and focus.
https://www.pexels.com/photo/kids-holding-colorful-balls-while-listening-to-their-teacher-8535234/

Active Listening Example 1

Because your child's baseball game starts at six, you won't have much time to help them prepare for the game while also having to supervise their study and cook as well. You start cooking dinner amidst the commotion while the kids play. You hear your son's crying all of a sudden. He approaches you and tells you that his brother slapped him and yelled at him. Although a part of you wants to carry on cooking while nodding along, you decide to actively listen instead and demonstrate to your son that you are totally focused. You stop what you're doing, turn to face him, make eye contact, and repeat his story along with his obvious emotions. You comment, "It seems like your brother's words and actions have upset you." Doing this demonstrates to your child that you are genuinely there and paying attention. You value his sentiments and emotions because they help you feel important and understand him better.

Active Listening Example 2

Your daughter is crying when you pick her up from preschool. She claims her friend stole her favorite toy and made fun of her by sticking out his tongue. You reply, "It sounds like you're feeling sad because your friend took your favorite toy," to show that you've been paying attention. She continues to cry while nodding in agreement. She goes on to worry that her friend could harm the toy after that. You continue to use an active listening strategy while acknowledging her feelings and asking, "So what's bothering you is that they might ruin your toy." Your daughter's misery starts to lessen a little bit over time. She understands as you two carry on talking that it's normal to feel unhappy. This contact is pivotal in her emotional development because it teaches her the value of expressing and managing her feelings.

Using Reflections to Show You're Listening

Reflection is useful for showing your child that you are paying close attention to what they are saying. This can be done by either restating their claims or summarizing and categorizing their feelings.

Reflections of Words

When you use word reflections, you acknowledge your child's expression and encourage further communication. You don't have to repeat their exact words, but your response usually closely resembles theirs. You might add details, simplify, or make corrections. Here's an example:

Child: "I drawed some sghetti."

Parent's Response: "So, you drew long *spaghetti.*"

In this case, the parent clarifies the pronunciation, improves the syntax, and provides additional information by referring to the spaghetti as "long."

Reflection of Emotions

Observing your child's behavior and articulating the feelings they appear to be feeling are both components of emotional reflection. This fosters the idea that talking about feelings is completely normal and teaches your child the language of emotions. Even though it may not always be easy to express feelings, here are some guidelines to help:

1. Take a Guess. Even if You Are Unsure

There will be instances when you're unsure about your child's emotions. For example, your child may be sobbing, but you're unsure whether they're upset, scared, or sad. When this happens, be sure to acknowledge it by saying something like, "It looks like you're bothered by something. " Talking to your child might help you both discover their sentiments because they might not always be conscious of them.

2. Words Aren't Needed All the Time

You can communicate your awareness of your child's emotions without uttering a word. Simply being present while your child is upset or maintaining physical closeness and offering comfort can convey your understanding.

3. You Don't Always Have to Agree

Summarizing or labeling your child's feelings can be challenging if you believe they should be reacting differently. However, urging your child to stop feeling a certain way doesn't demonstrate your efforts to comprehend their emotions. Instead, engage in conversations that help your child manage and grasp their feelings.

4. Talk about Other Feelings

Children often experience a mix of emotions simultaneously. For instance, your child might feel both sad and afraid. Express your concern for both the outward expressions and the potential inner feelings by discussing all the emotions they might be experiencing.

As you practice active listening, feeling concerned about getting your child's emotions right is okay. But don't worry too much. Children often let you know if you don't quite understand. If your child corrects you, that's a chance to learn together. Think about what they say and talk about it more. This can help them learn more words for their feelings and express themselves better.

Chapter 4: Building Emotional Intelligence

Most children aren't that great when it comes to emotional intelligence. Many find it hard to regulate their emotions and even recognize emotional cues. These skills don't come naturally to anyone, let alone young children. Your duty as a parent is to teach your children about feelings and emotions and how to deal with them healthily. The capacity of a youngster to express and regulate their emotions and feelings while also showing consideration for others is what emotional intelligence means. Emotional intelligence also includes a significant amount of empathy and compassion. Five components of emotional intelligence encompass both the individual and social facets:

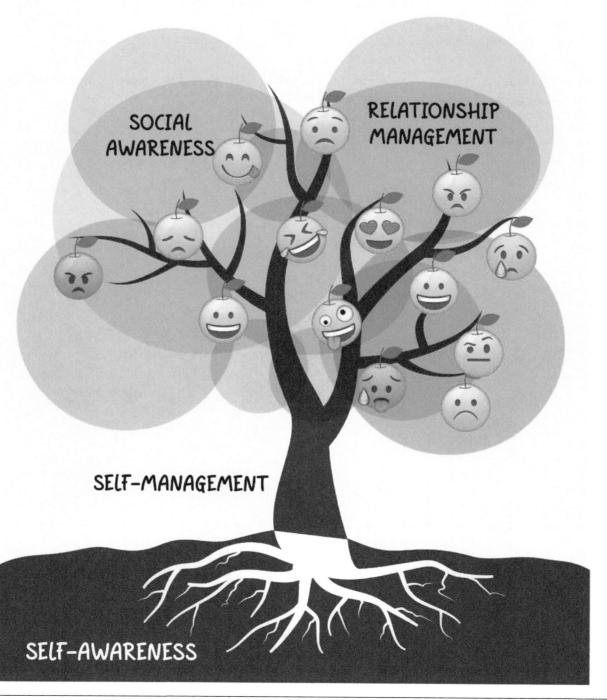

1. Self-awareness refers to a person's ability to comprehend their emotions, acknowledge their strengths and weaknesses, and grasp their impact on themselves and those around them.
2. Self-regulation, or self-management, refers to their aptitude for controlling their emotions, navigating through periods of change or stress, handling conflicts, and demonstrating adaptability and flexibility.
3. Self-motivation involves possessing the inner determination to fulfill their requirements and aspirations.
4. Social awareness refers to a person's capability to empathize with the emotions and needs of others.
5. Social skills encompass various abilities, including assertive communication and active listening, facilitating effective interaction and engagement with others.

It is your duty as a parent to teach your children about feelings and emotions and how to deal with them in a healthy way.
https://www.pexels.com/photo/photograph-of-a-therapist-showing-emotions-to-a-child-7447266/

How Emotional Intelligence Helps Resolve Conflicts

Emotional intelligence is not just something you need when you're older; it's a skill that should be developed from a young age. It makes your child perform better academically and helps them connect better with others, whether it's friends, classmates, teachers, or family members. Now, you're probably wondering how this helps with conflicts and arguments. Well, conflicts arise because of misunderstandings and unclear communication. Arguments can easily be resolved if someone is skilled enough to recognize and label their emotions instead of acting on them without thought.

For instance, say your child got into an argument with a classmate, and it's escalating fast. If they're not emotionally intelligent, they won't recognize that what they're feeling is anger and frustration. As a result, they'll act on their baser urges and might start a fight. Now, imagine if they could regulate their emotions healthily; they would recognize what they were feeling in the moment and try some calming techniques to control their anger.

Emotional intelligence combined with good communication skills is all your child needs to win arguments and resolve difficult situations. The plus side is that emotional intelligence skills can be taught to all kids. All they require is a teacher! Here's what you need to do:

• Label Their Emotions

Children greatly benefit from learning how to recognize and label their emotions. You can support your child by teaching them how to identify their feelings, especially when you have an idea of what they might be experiencing.

For example, you may say, "It seems like you might be feeling really furious right now. You might be upset over losing a game or having to share a toy. That's how you're feeling, right?" If someone seems dejected, you can enquire, "Could it be that you're feeling disappointed because we won't be able to visit your grandparents today?"

Words that reflect emotions, such as "shy," "angry," "hurt," and "upset," can all add to a person's vocabulary and help them communicate their sentiments. Also, don't forget to include words with positive emotions like "joyful," "excited," "thrilled," and "hopeful." Help your youngster identify the various emotions by using the provided feelings chart.

• Be Empathetic

When your child is feeling upset, it might be tempting to downplay their feelings. However, making dismissive remarks can convey that their emotions are invalid.

Even if you don't entirely comprehend why they're so upset, acknowledging their emotions and demonstrating empathy for them would be preferable. Say something like, "I understand what it means to feel a certain way when things don't go how we want them to," if your child is crying because you told them they need to clean up their room before going to the park.

When your child recognizes that you genuinely understand their inner feelings, they're less likely to resort to outward displays of emotion. Instead of shouting or crying to express their anger, they'll find comfort in knowing you're already aware of how they feel.

• Be a Role Model

Everyone has emotions; it's a universal truth. The difference between adults and children is that adults know how to express their emotions in a socially acceptable manner, whereas children tend to just throw around however they feel in any way possible. For instance, when children throw a tantrum, they often start hitting themselves or anyone around them. This unruly behavior cannot last them a lifetime, especially when they encounter conflicts. It is, therefore, crucial to teach them how to communicate what they're feeling in a healthy and socially acceptable manner. Even saying "I am upset" or making a sorrowful look can be beneficial, as opposed to yelling and hurling things, which is inappropriate behavior.

The most effective approach to teaching your child how to communicate their feelings is by doing it yourself. Start to use a vocabulary of emotions in your daily conversations and practice openly discussing feelings. You might say, "I feel frustrated when I witness unkindness in the playground," or "I feel joyful when we have our friends over for dinner."

- **Teach Healthy Coping Skills**

After you've taught your child to identify their emotions, you then need to guide them on how you handle these emotions in a healthy manner. They need to be able to relax, improve their mood, and face their fears. For this, you can teach them different techniques, particularly breathing techniques, to help them control their emotions. You could also create a personalized emotional regulation toolkit with your child. Include things like coloring books, some calming music, and scented lotions. These items will engage their senses and help them calm down. Remind them to use their calm-down kit whenever they are unhappy.

- **Develop Problem-Solving Skills**

Learning how to solve problems is an essential component of gaining emotional intelligence. Once your child has mastered labeling and addressing their emotions, it's time to educate them on how to resolve the underlying issue that gave rise to those challenging emotions in the first place. This will be particularly helpful when your child is facing a conflict. Let's say your child gets frustrated with their sibling for interrupting them when they are playing. Help them think of at least five solutions to this. The concepts don't need to be flawless. Getting them to brainstorm is the goal here. Once they've made a list, assist them in evaluating the advantages and disadvantages of each choice. Next, encourage them to choose the one that seems best.

Emotional Intelligence Activities

- **Emotion Charades**

Emotion charades can be a fun and engaging game for children. It teaches them about different emotions and the facial expressions that come with them. This way, your child can explore how they can express their emotions. You can use flashcards for this activity.

EMOTIONS CHARADES

HAPPY

SAD

ANGRY

SHOCKED

IN LOVE

BORED

CRYING

CONFUSED

TIRED

• **Emotion Drawing**

One of the simplest yet most effective activities for your child to learn how to identify different emotions is to draw them. Ask them to draw and color faces with different emotions. For younger children, these drawings can be as simple as emojis, but for older children, drawing with as much detail as possible is preferable.

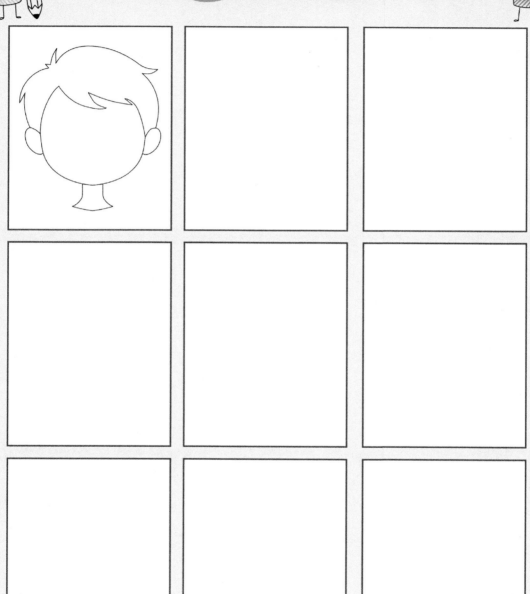

• Emotion Pictionary

Pictionary is a fun game just as it is, but add emotions to the mix, and you've got a great educational activity. You can play this game with your child or let them play with friends. Each player should draw a picture, and everyone else must guess the emotion. Use the given flashcards for the pictures!

HAPPINESS	SADNESS	ANGER
FEAR	SURPRISE	DISGUST
EXCITEMENT	LOVE	ANXIETY
TRUST	DISTRUST	HATE
JOY	SCARED	GRIEF
CURIOSITY	SURPRISE	GRATITUDE
PRIDE	COMPASSION	SHAME
SORROW	TIRED	ENTHUSIASM

EMOTIONS PICTIONARY

• Emotion Detective Worksheet

Have your child imagine that they are an emotion detective. Get them to look at each scenario below and choose the emotion that best matches how the person might be feeling. They should then draw a picture to show that emotion.

- **Scenario:** Jenny has lost her favorite toy.

Emotion:

- Sad
- Angry
- Happy
- Surprised

- **Scenario:** Tom is about to go on a fun roller coaster ride.

Emotion:
- Excited
- Scared
- Calm
- Proud

Draw the emotion:

- **Scenario:** Maria has received a special award for her good behavior.

Emotion:

- Happy
- Sad
- Nervous
- Proud

- **Scenario:** Alex has accidentally broken a plate.

Emotion:

- Angry
- Surprised
- Sad
- Excited

- **Scenario:** It's time to open birthday presents!

Emotion:

- Excited
- Nervous
- Calm
- Sad

- **Scenario:** Sarah is going to a new school for the first time.

Emotion:

- Nervous
- Happy
- Angry
- Scared

Draw the emotion:

- **Scenario:** Jake's best friend is moving away.

Emotion:
- Sad
- Excited
- Proud
- Angry

- **Scenario:** Emily saw a surprise gift waiting for her.

Emotion:

- Surprised
- Calm
- Happy
- Scared

Draw the emotion:

Remember, different people can feel different emotions in the same situation. Think about how each person might feel and have fun drawing their expressions!

- **Feelings Journal**

Keeping a journal is a wonderful technique for navigating emotions and nurturing emotional intelligence. Ask your child to take a few moments to think about their experiences each day. This practice can considerably improve children's ability to connect with others. Here are some journaling prompts they can start with:

1. Reflect on how you felt today. Were you happy, sad, excited, or something else? Write down why you think you felt that way.

2. Write about a time when you faced a challenge. How did you feel? What did you do to overcome it?

3. Recall something you did for someone or something kind someone did for you. How did it make you feel? Why is kindness important?

4. Think about a time when you felt really good. Describe that moment and why it made you feel so happy.

5. Write about a time when you felt upset. What did you do to calm down? Did talking to someone help? How could you handle it differently next time?

6. Describe something new you tried recently. How did you feel before, during, and after? What did you learn from this experience?

7. Imagine being in someone else's shoes. Write about a situation from their perspective. How might they feel? What could you do to help them?

8. Recall a special memory that brings you joy. Describe it in detail and explain why it's meaningful to you.

9. List activities that make you feel happy and calm. Choose one to do today and describe how it made you feel afterward.

• **Spot the Emotion**

Take a magazine or a photo book and see how many different emotions your child can identify. Encourage them to pinpoint and describe each specific emotion they find. How did they interpret and understand each emotion they found?

• **Coping Solutions**

In each situation, ask your child to think about how to cope with their feelings and improve the conflict.

Situation 1: You and your friend both want to use the same art supplies.

Solution:

_____

Situation 2: Your little sister accidentally tore a page from your favorite book.

Solution:

_____

Situation 3: You and your best friend had an argument.

Solution:

_____

Situation 4: You're nervous about giving a presentation in front of the class.

Solution:

_____

Situation 5: You're waiting for your turn to play a game, and it's taking a long time.

Solution:

_____

Remember, coping solutions are tools you can use to handle tough situations. By thinking ahead and coming up with ways to cope, you can make conflicts easier to manage for your child.

Emotional intelligence isn't just for grown-ups. Children can greatly benefit from it, too! Imagine conflict resolution as a puzzle. When children have good emotional skills, they can understand their feelings and figure out how others feel; thus, they can listen, think, and talk kindly when disagreements happen. This helps them solve problems and maintain friendships.

Chapter 5: A Step-by-Step Guide to Negotiation and Compromise

Arguments and conflicts are so common between children that you sometimes wonder why they haven't already mastered the art of negotiation or at least learned how to compromise. Like everything else, these skills have to be taught to children by their parents. They will not just help them during their childhood but also set the foundation for how they react to any future conflicts they have. While you want your child to be understanding and accommodating, you also don't want them to be so accommodating that they become a doormat. There is a very fine line between compromise and people-pleasing behavior. If you don't teach your child the difference between them, they will eventually become a pushover. This is where negotiation comes in. Learning negotiation skills helps children discover how to share and make fair decisions. Children start practicing these abilities early, like picking games with friends or agreeing on who gets to play with new toys. Sometimes, this involves arguments and fights, especially with siblings or friends. To help them learn to negotiate peacefully, you can teach them better ways to talk and understand each other.

There is a very fine line between compromise and people-pleasing behavior.
https://www.pexels.com/photo/brother-lying-together-on-a-bed-eating-a-fruit-8671139/

You've probably heard stories about college freshmen whose parents step in to negotiate for them as soon as they face challenges or disappointments. Whether "helicopter parenting" is as common as the media suggests, many parents want their children to learn how to stand up for themselves. This is especially important for girls who might feel pressure to always go along with others. While schools teach children how to solve conflicts, they don't always teach them how to negotiate effectively. These skills can help children ask for what they need and prevent problems. Even young children can understand basic negotiation ideas, like thinking about what to do if they don't get what they want and finding ways to make both sides happy. To teach them about negotiation, explain that it's a peaceful process where both sides treat each other well, no one is forced into anything, and everyone feels good about the outcome. Instead of just talking to them, try more subtle ways like:

• **Sibling Sharing Role-Play**

Imagine that you and your sibling each want the same candy flavor, and there's only one left. You have to work together to find a fair way to share it.

Think about why you both want the candy. Write down your reasons. For example, you might write, "I want the candy because it's my favorite flavor," or "I want the candy because I had a tough day."

Reasons:

   1. _____

   2. _____

   3. _____

Solutions:

Come up with three different ways to share the candy. For example:

• You each get half.

• You trade something else for candy.

• You take turns having it for a certain amount of time.

• _____

• _____

• _____

Act out each solution with your sibling. Take turns being each other and discussing which option feels the most fair. Choose the solution that you both think is the fairest and explain why. Write down your final decision and how you feel about it.

Decision:

_____

Reflection:

• Was it hard to compromise? Why or why not?

   _____

• What did you learn about negotiating and sharing?

   _____

• How could you use these skills in other situations?

   _____

Remember, negotiating is about finding a solution that makes everyone feel good.

• Team Project Role-Play

Imagine that you and your friends have to work together on a team project, but you all have different ideas. The key is negotiating and collaborating to create an amazing final product that combines everyone's unique contributions. Form small teams of 3-4 people. Each team member will have a different role in the project. Give each team member a few minutes to develop their ideas for the project. Have each team member share their ideas with the group. Discuss the pros and cons of each idea and how they could be combined to make something even better.

As a team, decide on the main concept for the project. Each team member should contribute their ideas and be willing to compromise. Divide the tasks needed to complete the project among team members. Work together to bring the project to life. Communicate openly, share ideas, and make decisions as a team. If disagreements arise, use negotiation skills to find solutions everyone agrees on. Once the project is complete, present it to the rest of the group. Explain how you collaborated, compromised, and combined your ideas to create a unified final product.

Reflection:

• How did you feel while negotiating and collaborating?

_____

• What were the challenges you faced, and how did you overcome them?

_____

• What did you learn about working in a team and valuing different perspectives?

_____

• Game-Based Learning
   o **Monopoly:** A classic board game that requires players to negotiate property trades and deals and even form alliances to succeed.

Monopoly can teach your child how to negotiate.

- o **The Game of Life:** This game involves making choices about careers, family, and finances, often requiring players to negotiate or compromise.
  - o **Pictionary:** Children work in teams to draw and guess words, promoting negotiation and communication skills.
  - o **Escape Room Challenges:** Participate in child-friendly escape room puzzles that require teamwork, negotiation, and problem-solving.
- • **Thumbs Up, Thumbs Down**

Negotiation Scenario:

_____

_____

Thumbs Up:

(Circle or Write Aspects that Went Well)

- • Effective Communication
- • Compromise
- • Respectful Behavior
- • Understanding Different Views
- • Problem-Solving

Thumbs Down:

(Circle or Write Areas for Improvement)

1. Lack of Patience
2. Ignoring Ideas
3. Getting Upset
4. Not Compromising
5. Interrupting

Strategies for Improvement:

(Write at Least One Strategy for Each Thumbs Down Aspect)

Lack of Patience:

Strategy: _____

Ignoring Ideas:

Strategy: _____

Getting Upset:

Strategy: _____

Not Compromising:

Strategy: _____

Interrupting:

Strategy: _____

Reflection Questions:

1. How did it feel to reflect on your negotiation experience using "Thumbs Up, Thumbs Down"?

   _____

2. What strategies do you think will help you become a better negotiator in the future?

   _____

3. How can you apply these negotiation skills to other areas of your life, like school or friendships?

   _____

- **Storytelling**

In this activity, you'll create a story where characters face a conflict and must negotiate a solution. Afterward, you'll discuss the negotiation tactics used and explore alternative ways the characters could have resolved the conflict.

Step 1: Setting the Scene

Think of a conflict for your story. It could be about sharing, choosing a game, or any other situation where characters have different desires.

_____
_____
_____
_____
_____
_____
_____
_____

Step 2: Character Creation

Create two characters who will be involved in the conflict. Give them names, ages, and a brief description of their personalities.

Character 1	Character 2

Step 3: Story Development

Write or tell the story of how the characters encounter the conflict and how they negotiate to find a solution. Be creative with the details and dialogue.

_____

_____

_____

_____

_____

_____

Step 4: Discussion of Negotiation Tactics

After sharing your story, discuss the negotiation tactics the characters used to resolve the conflict. Talk about what went well and what could have been done differently.

_____

_____

_____

_____

_____

_____

Step 5: Exploring Alternatives

Imagine alternative ways in which the characters could have negotiated. What if they tried a different approach? Discuss how these alternatives might have affected the outcome.

_____

_____

_____

_____

_____

Step 6: Role-Playing Alternatives

Take turns acting out the alternative negotiation scenarios. Play the characters and try negotiating using the different tactics you discussed.

_____

_____

_____

_____

_____

Step 7: Reflection and Learning

How did it feel to create a story about negotiation and conflict resolution?

_____

What negotiation tactics did the characters use effectively?

_____

How did the alternative negotiation scenarios change the outcome of the story?

_____

What Is Compromise?

Compromising is all about finding a middle ground or adjusting your stance to come to an agreement. Some parents never change their minds – something they end up inadvertently modeling for their children. However, as children grow older, parents should be open to negotiating. When children reach school age, it's okay for rules to be up for discussion. If both you and your rules are fair, you can talk about them. Negotiating doesn't mean you're weak. It actually stems from being confident in your authority. The focus of negotiation is the rule itself, not your parental control. Instead of demanding obedience, it's better to say, "Convince me." If they have good reasons, consider changing the rule.

Sometimes, you shouldn't compromise; for instance, bad words, lying, and stealing should *never be negotiable*. Children must understand that compromise doesn't mean giving up important values for peace. How you show compromise in your relationship teaches them about principles and their self-worth. Children start learning about compromise during play, often with siblings. They might argue over toys, movies, clothes, or seats in the car. These situations are common, and it's natural to feel stressed. Your goal is to help them handle these situations on their own.

Personality also plays a role in how children handle conflicts. Some are confident and argue, while others avoid conflict. But as children grow up, they need to learn to compromise. Think about all the things you do just because you feel you should or how hard it is to say "no" to others. Teaching a healthy way to compromise is important for becoming a well-rounded adult.

• It's Healthy to Argue

It's actually healthy for children to argue sometimes. Instead of shutting them down, help them learn how to argue in a positive way. Do that by teaching them how to negotiate their points. For instance, if they want to stay up late to watch a show, encourage them to make a good case for why they should be allowed to do so. They should explain what they want, why they think it's reasonable, and what they're willing to compromise on. If their argument makes sense, consider being open to negotiation. You could say something like: "You know, it's okay to have disagreements sometimes. It's a chance to learn and grow." Or, "Let's practice talking about why you want something and what you're willing to give in return. This is a great way to find common ground."

• Win-Win

A "win-win" approach should be taken. This means that both sides involved in the argument should be ready to give up something to get what they want. For example, if two children are arguing over a toy, they can take turns playing with it or find a way to play together. Or, if one child gets to choose the movie today, they might have to watch their sibling's choice tomorrow. When both sides make compromises, it prevents lingering hard feelings. Talk to your child, and say something along the lines of

"When we have different ideas, it's a chance to find a solution that works for both of us." Or, "Choosing together can be really fun. You get to make a choice today, and they get a turn tomorrow. That's a fair way to do things." Or even, "When both sides give a little, everyone feels happy and satisfied."

- **Empathy**

Empathy is another crucial aspect. While children naturally focus on their own wants and needs, they should develop an understanding of how their actions affect others. When your child is in an argument, encourage them to pause and think about the other person's perspective: How does their desire impact the other person? What might the other person be feeling? Ask them, "Imagine if you were in their position. How would you want to be treated?" Or, "When you argue, think about how your decision might affect the other person. It's important to consider their feelings, too."

Learning how to compromise is a skill that takes practice. Undoubtedly, children can greatly benefit from guidance in managing their emotions during conflicts, which ultimately enables them to find common ground. Once shown both perspectives, children readily embrace mutual give-and-take, forgiving, and moving on.

Chapter 6: From Conflict to Collaboration

Collaborating, or the win-win approach to conflict, is perhaps the best approach. Although everyone has a different preference for conflict resolution, there's no better way to solve a problem than by ensuring that both parties come out of it satisfied. Although the compromise approach promises peaceful results, it does not consider the person's inner satisfaction. Most people who opt for this approach are people-pleasers, although there are exceptions.

Collaboration Vs. Compromise

Collaboration means working together to find solutions that make everyone happy. Instead of just giving in a little bit (compromising), collaboration looks at what each person really wants. When people collaborate, they talk openly, listen to each other, and think of new ideas. This helps them find better answers than if they were working alone. It's not about winning or losing but about everyone feeling good about the outcome. Collaboration is great because it helps build stronger relationships and makes people trust each other more. Even though it might not work for every situation, when it does work, it leads to creative solutions and everyone feeling satisfied.

When people collaborate, they talk openly, listen to each other, and think of new ideas.
https://www.pexels.com/photo/cheerful-group-of-teenagers-using-laptop-7869229/

Shifting your child's attitude from combative to calm can be game-changing when it comes to handling conflicts. Encouraging collaboration and teamwork within your family will set the stage for positive outcomes that benefit everyone involved. Imagine the difference it could make if you could avoid those tense standoffs and instead work together toward solutions that satisfy you and your child. Say your child wants to stay up late to watch their favorite TV show, but you know it's important for them to get enough sleep. Instead of getting into an argument, you could shift the conversation to a collaborative one. You might say, "I understand you want to watch your show, and I want you to get enough rest. How about we find a solution we both want, like watching half of it now and the rest tomorrow after you finish your homework?" This approach not only addresses their desire but also considers their responsibilities.

Teaching Your Child Collaboration

When you foster a collaborative frame of mind, you're resolving immediate conflicts and shaping your child's future relationships. When they learn that working together and considering others' perspectives leads to better outcomes, they'll carry this valuable lesson into their interactions outside the family. Imagine your child disagreeing with a friend over choosing a game to play. Instead of arguing, they might suggest, "How about we take turns picking games? That way, we both get a chance to play something we enjoy."

Furthermore, the shift from combative to collaborative thinking instills mutual respect and understanding in your child. They learn to appreciate that everyone's opinions matter and that compromise can be a win-win situation. Just like when they wanted to go to the park, you had other plans. Instead of sulking, they could propose, "Can we go to the park today and do what you suggested tomorrow?" This way, they learn to communicate their desires while considering yours. As parents, it's natural to want what's best for your children. Teaching them to approach conflicts collaboratively gives them a lifelong tool for building healthy relationships, effective communication, and empathy. This shift transforms how you handle daily challenges and lays the foundation for your child's future success in personal and professional interactions. Here are some ways you can help them take the collaborative approach whenever there's a conflict:

• Group Art Project

In this activity, you'll craft a visual mood board with the help of your friends. You will need to share ideas, compromise, and combine your unique styles.

Materials Needed:

- • Magazines, newspapers, or printed images
- • Scissors
- • Glue or sticky tape
- • Poster board or a designated space for your mood board
- • Markers, colored pencils, or other decorative materials

Instructions:

Gather your friends and decide on a theme for your mood board. Here are some theme ideas to consider:

1. Adventure Awaits.
2. My Superpowers.
3. Nature's Wonders.
4. Future Careers.
5. Friendship Forever.

Next, sit down together and share your thoughts about the chosen theme. Answer the following questions individually and then discuss your answers as a group:

What does this theme mean to you?

_____

What images, words, and colors come to mind when you think about this theme?

_____

How can we represent this theme visually on our mood board?

_____

Write down the theme ideas of each person in the given table:

Name	Selected Theme

After discussing the theme ideas, vote as a group to choose the final theme for your mood board. Write down the chosen theme below:

Chosen Theme: _____

Image and Word Selection:

Name	Selected Images and Words

Discuss the images and words each person chose. Are there any overlaps or similarities? How can you compromise to ensure everyone's ideas are included in the mood board?

Using a separate sheet of paper, sketch a rough layout of how you want to arrange the images and words on the mood board. Consider where you will place each element and how they will work together.

Start assembling the mood board together. Encourage each friend to add their cutouts and decorative touches. How can you arrange the elements to create a visually appealing and balanced composition?

• Building Challenge

In this exciting activity, you and your friends will use building materials like LEGO, blocks, or cardboard to create an amazing structure or design. Get ready to flex your problem-solving muscles and experience the thrill of collaboration!

• Storytelling Circle

In this activity, you'll sit in a circle with your friends and work together to narrate a captivating tale. With each person contributing a sentence or two, you'll get to spark your imagination, boost creativity, and experience the joy of cooperative storytelling.

Gather your friends and decide on the setting for your collaborative story. Here are some exciting ideas to consider:

- **Enchanted Forest**: A magical world filled with talking animals and hidden treasures.

- **Space Adventure:** Explore the universe, encounter aliens, and travel to distant planets.

- **Under the Sea:** Dive into the ocean's depths and meet underwater creatures on a thrilling journey.

Dive into the depths of the ocean and meet underwater creatures on a thrilling journey.
https://pixabay.com/vectors/shark-diver-megalodon-periscope-6942486/

- **Time Travel Quest:** Venture through different time periods to solve mysteries and discover ancient secrets.

Discuss the story setting options as a group and cast your votes to choose the most exciting one. Write down the chosen setting below:

Chosen Setting: _____

To begin the story, one friend will begin by sharing a sentence that introduces the setting and the main character. What is the first sentence of your collaborative story?

_____
_____
_____

Sitting in a circle, take turns adding to the story. Each child contributes a sentence or two to continue the narrative. Remember to listen to your friends' ideas as the story unfolds and build upon their contributions. Keep writing down everyone's additions:

- _____
_____
- _____
_____

- _____
  _____
- _____
  _____
- _____
  _____
- _____
  _____

As the story reaches the end, work together to build tension and excitement. Then, collaboratively conclude the story with a satisfying resolution. How will your characters overcome challenges and bring the story to a close?

_____
_____
_____
_____

Reflect on your collaborative storytelling experience. Answer the following questions individually and then share your thoughts as a group:

- How did working together to create a story enhance your creativity and cooperation?

  _____

- What were some of your favorite moments or sentences in the collaborative story?

  _____

- How did each person's contributions make the story more interesting and engaging?

  _____

- **Science Experiment**

In this activity, you and your friends will work together to conduct a simple yet fascinating science experiment. Assign different roles to everyone and coordinate your actions so you'll develop teamwork skills while unraveling the mysteries of science. Here are some experiments you can try:

Baking Soda and Vinegar Volcano

You'll Need:

- An empty plastic bottle
- Baking soda
- Vinegar
- Dish soap (optional, for added frothy fun)
- Red food coloring (optional, for lava effect)
- Safety goggles (to protect your eyes)

Choose Roles for Each Friend:

- Pourer: Put the baking soda into the bottle.
- Vinegar Splasher: Pour vinegar into the bottle.
- Lava Watcher: Observe the bubbling reaction.
- Photographer: Capture the exciting moment.

Instructions:

1. Pour some baking soda into the bottle (about two tablespoons).
2. Add a few drops of food coloring to the vinegar if you want red lava.
3. Carefully pour vinegar into the bottle (about half full).
4. Watch the bubbly eruption and see the "lava" flow down!

Observations:

- How did the baking soda and vinegar create bubbles?

  _____

- Did the red food coloring make the "lava" more realistic?

  _____

- How did each role contribute to the experiment's success?

  _____

(**Note:** Adult supervision is recommended when handling vinegar and baking soda.)

Experiment: Rainbow Magic with Water and Food Coloring

You'll Need:

- Clear cups or jars
- Water
- Food coloring (red, blue, yellow)
- Small spoons for stirring

Choose Roles for Each Friend:

- Color Master: Add food coloring drops to cups.
- Water Mixer: Pour water into the cups.
- Stirring Magician: Mix the colors to create the rainbow.

Instructions:

1. Fill the cups with water, about halfway full.
2. Add a few drops of red food coloring to one cup, blue to another, and yellow to the third.
3. Use a separate spoon to take small amounts of each color and gently stir together to see the magic happen!

Observations:

How did the primary colors (red, blue, yellow) mix to create new colors?

_____

What happened when you stirred the colors together?

_____

How did each role contribute to the rainbow's creation?

_____

- **Cooking or Baking**

In this activity, you and your friends will collaborate to create a yummy and colorful layered parfait. Each one will have a special role in making this delightful dessert come to life.

Ingredients:

- Greek yogurt (vanilla or plain).
- Assorted fresh fruits (berries, bananas, kiwi, etc.).
- Granola or crushed cereal.
- Honey or maple syrup (optional).
- Clear glasses or bowls for layering.

Choose Roles for Each Friend:

- The Fruit Master: Wash, peel, and cut the fruits.

  _____

- The Layering Pro: Add layers of yogurt, fruits, and granola.

  _____

- The Drizzler: Add a touch of honey or maple syrup (if desired).

  _____

- The Presentation Artist: Make the parfaits look extra pretty!

  _____

Discuss the choice of fruits, layering order, and whether you want to drizzle honey or maple syrup.

Name	Chosen Fruits	Layering Order	Drizzle Preference

Follow your layering plan to create beautiful parfaits. Each person takes their turn to add yogurt, fruits, and granola to the clear glasses or bowls.

The Drizzler adds a touch of sweetness by gently drizzling honey or maple syrup over the top of each parfait.

The Presentation Artist makes the parfaits look fantastic! Arrange fruits on top or sprinkle a little extra granola to make them picture-perfect.

- **Group Games**

Play games encouraging cooperation and teamwork, such as relay races, tug-of-war, or three-legged races. These activities emphasize the importance of coordinated efforts.

- **Role-Playing Game**

Play this fun role-playing game in which you and your friends embark on an adventure-filled journey.

Once upon a time, a mighty kingdom stood in a land where magic flowed like rivers. The kingdom's prosperity relied on the power of a sacred crystal known as the Crystal of Harmony. This crystal, hidden deep within the Enchanted Forest, maintained balance and peace across the realm.

However, one day, a dark sorcerer sought to steal the Crystal of Harmony for his own malevolent purposes. The kingdom was thrown into turmoil as the crystal's magic waned, and nature itself became chaotic.

The kingdom's leaders called upon a group of courageous heroes to retrieve the crystal and restore balance to the land. These heroes were no ordinary adventurers – they possessed unique skills and abilities that made them the realm's last hope.

Characters:

- Sir Galan the Brave Knight: Known for his swordsmanship and courage.
- Merlin the Wise Wizard: A master of spells and knowledge.
- Elena the Curious Explorer: A skilled tracker and expert in uncovering mysteries.
- Luna the Friendly Forest Sprite: Communicates with animals and possesses woodland magic.
- Finn the Resourceful Inventor: Creates gadgets and devices.

Gather your friends and read the story of "The Enchanted Crystal of Harmony" together. Imagine the kingdom, the forest, and the heroes' quest to retrieve the crystal. Discuss the story elements: the kingdom's crisis, the sacred crystal, the heroes' abilities, and the challenges they face. How can your team of heroes work together to overcome obstacles and save the realm?

Assign Characters:

Assign each friend a character role:

1. Sir Galan the Brave Knight: _____
2. Merlin the Wise Wizard: _____
3. Elena the Curious Explorer: _____
4. Luna the Friendly Forest Sprite: _____
5. Finn the Resourceful Inventor: _____

The Quest:

Divide the story into key scenes and act them out as a team. Each person portrays their character and contributes to the narrative's progression. Discuss and record how characters interact in each scene. How do their unique abilities complement one another, and how do they make decisions as a team?

_____
_____
_____
_____

_____

_____

_____

Conclude the role-play with the heroes successfully retrieving the Crystal of Harmony and restoring balance to the realm. How did their teamwork and character skills contribute to the quest's success?

_____

_____

_____

_____

Chapter 7: The Art of Problem-Solving

Problem-solving is simply the process of finding a solution to a problem, a complex issue, or a challenging situation. Cognitive skills, which serve as a framework for problem-solving, start developing from an early age. Your child will use their experience, knowledge, and information to try to solve the problem and reach a solution. Depending on the severity of the problem, your child will use analytical thinking, decision-making, logical reasoning, communication, reasoning, creativity, and lateral thinking to find a feasible solution. While some children are naturally good at solving problems, others require support and encouragement from their parents and caregivers to get started.

The Process of Problem Solving

Identify the Issue

The first step a parent or a primary caregiver could adopt is understanding the problems a child is facing. They might be having difficulty doing homework, feeling upset about a situation, or not getting along with a friend. Ask your child questions to learn more about what's happening. This helps you clearly understand what's happening in their life and what they're feeling. If they are hesitant to share, observe them closely to try to figure out what's disturbing them.

Brainstorm Solutions

Sit down with your child and think of different ways to tackle the problem. Encourage them to share their ideas, offer your own, and write down a list. Make the effort to get it to feel like it's just another family activity.

Evaluate Options

Look at the list of ideas you've come up with. Let your child pick the possible solutions, and after they are done, you can suggest they choose other ideas that work best for their situation. Now, talk about the pros and cons of each one to further filter out the best possible solution.

Choose a Solution

After discussing the options, decide together which solution to try first. Make sure your child feels involved in the decision-making process.

Make a Plan

Break down the chosen solution into steps. Help your child understand what needs to be done. For example, suppose the problem is getting ready for school on time. In that case, the plan might include setting an alarm, picking out clothes the night before, and having breakfast ready.

Put the Plan into Action

Support your child as they put the plan into action. Provide guidance and encouragement.

Monitor Progress

Keep an eye on how things are going. If the solution is working, that's fantastic! If not, don't worry. It's okay to make adjustments or try a different approach.

Celebrate Successes

When your child makes progress or successfully solves the problem, celebrate! It could be as simple as giving them a high-five or acknowledging their effort. Positive reinforcement builds their confidence.

Reflect and Learn

After some time, talk with your child about what worked and what didn't. Reflect on the experience together. This teaches them that learning from challenges is essential and that having some of the answers is okay.

Strategies to Improve Problem Solving

1. Encourage Curiosity

Encouraging curiosity means supporting your child's natural eagerness to learn and explore. When they ask questions about things they're curious about, take the time to answer or find resources that can provide more information. You can read books, watch videos, or visit places related to your interests. This helps them develop a habit of seeking solutions and understanding the world around them.

Example of a Real-Life Scenario: Say your child looks up at the sky and asks, "Why is the sky blue?" Instead of simply providing an answer, you take the opportunity to encourage their curiosity. You reply, "That's a great question! The sky looks blue because sunlight interacts with the air molecules in our atmosphere. I'm sure you want to learn more! Let's read about it."

2. Provide Challenges

Offering challenges involves providing activities that stimulate your child's thinking and creativity. Choose puzzles, games, and appropriate tasks for their age and developmental level. These challenges should be engaging enough to capture their interest but not so difficult that they become frustrated. As they work through these challenges, they develop problem-solving skills by experimenting with different approaches and strategies.

Example of a Real-Life Scenario: You decide to challenge your child's problem-solving skills by giving them a jigsaw puzzle that's a bit more complex than the ones they usually do. You say, "I have a special puzzle for you today! It might be a bit trickier, but I believe in your ability to solve it. Take your time. I'm here to help if you need me."

3. Avoid Immediate Solutions

When your child faces a problem, resist the urge to give them a solution immediately. Instead, encourage them to think about the issue and possible solutions themselves. Ask open-ended questions that guide their thinking, such as "What options do you have?" or "How do you think you could solve this?" This approach empowers them to think critically and come up with solutions independently.

Example of a Real-Life Scenario: Your child is frustrated because they can't figure out how to assemble a new toy. Instead of stepping in to solve it, you kneel down and ask, "Hmm, it looks like you're having some trouble. What do you think could be causing the problem? Is there a certain part that seems tricky?"

4. Teach Them the Steps of Problem-Solving

Break down problem-solving into four steps: understanding the problem, making a plan, trying it, and checking if it works. Use relatable examples from their experiences to explain each step. For instance, you could discuss how they plan their playtime, which involves understanding what they want to do, deciding how to do it, actually playing, and seeing if they enjoy it afterward.

Example of a Real-Life Scenario: Your child faces a challenging math problem that stumps them. You guide them through the process of solving that problem by saying, "Let's work on this math problem together. First, let's make sure we understand what the question is. Then, we can devise a plan to solve it step by step."

5. Use Real-Life Scenarios

Introduce real-life situations that include challenges your child might encounter. You could talk about sharing toys with friends or deciding which game to play. Discuss the different ways they could approach these situations and the potential outcomes of each choice. This helps them practice problem-solving skills in contexts that are meaningful to them.

Example of a Real-Life Scenario: Your child comes home from school upset because their friend borrowed a toy without asking. You sit with them and say, "I'm sorry to hear that happened. Let's discuss how you could handle this situation if it happens again. How can we solve this problem together?"

6. Brainstorm Together

Including your child in brainstorming sessions will help them think creatively.
https://unsplash.com/photos/Ax8IA8GAjVg?utm_source=unsplash&utm_medium=referral&utm_content=creditShareLink

Engage your child in brainstorming sessions in which you both generate ideas to address a problem. This teaches them to think creatively and consider multiple options. As you brainstorm, encourage them to share their thoughts and help them evaluate the pros and cons of different ideas. This collaborative approach fosters teamwork and a sense of shared problem-solving.

Example of a Real-Life Scenario: On a rainy day, your child looks bored and unsure of what to do. You sit down with them and say, "Rainy days can be a bit challenging, but we can brainstorm some fun indoor activities together. What are some ideas you have?"

7. Embrace Mistakes

Create an environment where making mistakes is seen as a natural part of learning. Share stories about when you made mistakes and how you used them to improve. When your child faces setbacks or errors, offer encouragement and emphasize that learning from mistakes is important. This helps them develop a growth mentality and the confidence to tackle challenges without fear of failure.

Example of a Real-Life Scenario: Your child accidentally spills paint while working on an art project. You reassure them by saying, "Oops, it looks like there's been a little spill. That's okay, mistakes happen. Let's clean it up together and talk about how we can avoid spills next time."

8. Provide Autonomy

Give your child opportunities to make decisions within certain boundaries. You could let them choose what to do after school or what book to read before bedtime. This gives them the chance to learn how to evaluate options, make choices, and take responsibility for their decisions, which are essential problem-solving skills.

Example of a Real-Life Scenario: You lay out a banana and an apple during snack time. You say, "It's snack time! You get to choose between the banana and the apple. Which one would you like to have today?"

9. Foster Critical Thinking

Encourage critical thinking by asking thought-provoking questions and encouraging your child to analyze situations from different angles. For example, ask, "Why do you think that happened?" or "What could be another way to solve this?" This habit of considering various perspectives enhances their problem-solving abilities.

Example of a Real-Life Scenario: Your child and their friend can't agree on which game to play together. You step in and say, "I can see you both have different ideas. How about we think of a few options and discuss each game's pros and cons? That might help you decide."

10. Model Problem Solving

When you encounter a problem, think out loud and explain your thought process to your child. Narrate how you approach the issue, the strategies you're considering, and the reasons behind your decisions. This provides a concrete example of how problem-solving works in real life and encourages them to apply similar approaches.

Example of a Real-Life Scenario: You can't find your keys when you're getting ready to leave the house. You think aloud, "Hmm, I remember having my keys in the kitchen earlier. Let's retrace my steps and think about where I might have put them."

11. Celebrate Efforts

Have your children focus their efforts on solving a problem instead of solely on the outcome. When they work hard, persist, and use creative thinking, acknowledge and praise their dedication. This gets them to associate their efforts with positive outcomes, reinforcing their willingness to tackle challenges.

Example of a Real-Life Scenario: Your child struggles to tie their shoelaces for the first time. You offer encouragement, saying, "I can see you're really focusing and trying your best to tie your shoelaces. That's fantastic! Keep practicing, and you'll get better over time."

12. Encourage Collaboration

Set up activities that require collaboration with others to solve a problem. You could work together to build a puzzle, create a craft project, or cook a meal. Collaborative problem-solving teaches your child how to communicate, share ideas, and consider different viewpoints to reach a solution.

Example of a Real-Life Scenario: Your child and their sibling want to build a fort together. You suggest, "How about you two work together to design and build a fort? It's a great opportunity to collaborate and develop creative ideas."

13. Provide Tools

Offer materials and tools that encourage hands-on problem-solving. Building blocks, art supplies, science kits, and other resources allow your child to experiment, create, and find solutions through hands-on exploration.

Example of a Real-Life Scenario: Your child is eager to build something with their blocks. You hand them various shapes and sizes and say, "Here are different blocks you can use to build. What kind of structure can you create with these?"

14. Read Problem-Solving Stories

Choose books that feature characters facing challenges and solving them creatively. After reading, discuss the characters' decisions, their strategies, and how they relate to your child's experiences.

Example of a Real-Life Scenario: You read a book with your child about characters working together to fix a broken toy. Afterward, you discuss the story: "Those characters had to solve a problem together. Can you think of a time when you worked with someone to solve a problem?"

Remember, these strategies are meant to be integrated into everyday interactions and activities. Consistent application of these approaches helps children develop problem-solving skills that will serve them well throughout the rest of their lives.

MAZES

Chapter 8: Tolerance, Understanding and Respect

Besides nurturing your child and providing the right care, you need to instill in them the fundamental values of understanding, respect, and tolerance. These core values empower children to tackle situations effectively and diminish escalating conflicts. Fostering a culture of tolerance lets your child embrace diversity, develop an open mind, be non-judgmental, and express empathy. Likewise, developing the core value of understanding in children makes them active listeners, enabling them to engage in meaningful conversations and seek common ground to reduce misunderstanding. Lastly, instilling respect enables the child to tackle complex interactions with wisdom and grace easily, mitigating the intensity and frequency of conflicts they might encounter as they slowly transition toward adulthood.

These core values empower children to tackle situations effectively and diminish escalating conflicts.

Tolerance

Tolerance is accepting and embracing differences, even when they contradict one's beliefs or values. It involves an open-minded and non-judgmental approach towards individuals with diverse cultural, social, or ideological backgrounds. Tolerance does not require agreement. It signifies a willingness to co-exist harmoniously with those who hold different perspectives. By fostering tolerance, children learn to appreciate the richness of diversity and develop a sense of empathy that enables them to engage constructively with people from varied walks of life. Tolerance teaches children to rise above biases and prejudices, creating an environment where everyone is treated with fairness and respect, regardless of their differences.

Understanding

Understanding involves actively seeking to understand the thoughts, emotions, and motivations of others. It goes beyond superficial interactions and encourages individuals, including children, to invest time and effort in exploring the reasons behind people's actions and viewpoints. Developing understanding requires effective communication and active listening, where children learn to ask questions, engage in meaningful conversations, and place themselves in others' shoes. This skill allows them to navigate disagreements with empathy and patience as they grasp the underlying factors that shape different perspectives. Ultimately, understanding fosters a deeper connection and promotes the resolution of conflicts through mutual comprehension and shared insights.

Respect

Respect hinges on acknowledging every individual's inherent worth and dignity, irrespective of their background, beliefs, or choices. It involves treating others with consideration, politeness, and fairness. For children, respect manifests as being mindful of their words and actions and refraining from behaviors that belittle or demean others. It extends to valuing personal boundaries, privacy, and autonomy. By practicing respect, children learn to create an atmosphere of trust and cooperation where people feel valued and empowered. Respect reinforces the idea that all individuals have a right to be heard and treated with kindness, promoting an inclusive environment that reduces the likelihood of conflicts stemming from disrespect or mistreatment.

Exploring Connectedness

Tolerance and understanding share a symbiotic relationship in which one complements and enhances the other. Tolerance is the initial step towards fostering understanding, as it establishes an environment where diverse viewpoints are acknowledged and respected. By embracing tolerance, individuals create a space conducive to open dialogue and exchanging ideas. This, in turn, encourages others to express themselves authentically, leading to a deeper understanding of the motivations and emotions underlying differing perspectives. As people engage in conversations with a tolerant mindset, they become more inclined to seek common ground and bridge gaps in comprehension, thereby reducing the potential for conflicts rooted in miscommunication or bias.

Understanding, in its essence, forms a bridge to respect, facilitating a profound connection between individuals. When people invest time and effort in genuinely understanding each other's experiences, struggles, and beliefs, they cultivate a sense of empathy and compassion. This empathetic understanding lays the groundwork for respect by highlighting every individual's intrinsic worth and uniqueness. As individuals appreciate the complexities of others' lives, they naturally develop a more profound respect for their diverse backgrounds and perspectives. This respect is grounded in a genuine acknowledgment of each person's value, fostering an atmosphere of inclusivity and reducing the likelihood of conflicts arising from disrespect or dismissiveness.

Respect, in turn, reinforces the practice of tolerance, creating a cycle of mutual acceptance and appreciation. When individuals treat each other with consideration, courtesy, and fairness, they establish a foundation that encourages the open expression of differing viewpoints. In a respectful environment, individuals feel comfortable sharing their thoughts without fear of judgment or exclusion. This sense of safety and acceptance encourages the practice of tolerance as individuals learn to value and embrace the differences that make each person unique. Children nurtured in an atmosphere of respect are more likely to approach interactions with an open heart and an eagerness to learn from others, thereby reducing the potential for conflicts arising from intolerance or bias.

The interconnectedness of tolerance, understanding, and respect forms a harmonious cycle that contributes to healthy relationships and effective conflict resolution. Tolerance facilitates understanding, understanding nurtures respect, and respect reinforces tolerance, creating a framework that empowers children to navigate conflicts with empathy, maturity, and a commitment to fostering peaceful coexistence.

When people invest time and effort in genuinely understanding each other's experiences, struggles, and beliefs, they cultivate a sense of empathy and compassion.
https://pixabay.com/photos/different-nationalities-children-1743392/

Practical Strategies to Instill Core Values

Exposure to Diversity

As a parent, you should expose your children to various cultures, traditions, and perspectives through activities such as cultural festivals, international cuisine nights, or visits to museums. By immersing children in different experiences, they appreciate the richness of human diversity.

Example of a Real-Life Scenario: A family decides to attend a cultural fair in their community, where they explore booths showing various traditions, try new foods, and engage in conversations with people from different backgrounds. This exposure sparks curiosity and prompts questions, leading to valuable discussions about different ways of life and the importance of embracing diversity.

Modeling Behavior

Children learn best through observation, so parents must model respectful behavior at home. You should demonstrate active listening, empathy, and kindness in your interactions with family members.

Example of a Real-Life Scenario: A child witnesses their parent engaging in a thoughtful conversation with a neighbor who holds differing political views. The parent listens attentively, asks questions, and maintains a respectful tone throughout the discussion. Later, the parent explains to the child that respectful communication is key to understanding each other and maintaining positive relationships even when people disagree.

Open Discussions

You need to initiate open-ended conversations about differences and encourage your children to ask questions without fear of judgment. These discussions provide opportunities to emphasize the value of respect and understanding.

Example of a Real-Life Scenario: A family is watching a news segment about refugees fleeing their home country. The parents pause the TV and engage their children in a conversation about why people might have to leave their homes, their challenges, and the importance of helping others in need. Through this dialogue, the parents emphasize the significance of empathy and the role understanding plays in supporting those facing difficult circumstances.

Storytelling and Media

Use books, movies, and TV shows that highlight diverse characters and themes as a means to spark conversations about tolerance and respect.

Example of a Real-Life Scenario: A family reads a book together about a character from a different cultural background who overcomes challenges and makes new friends. Afterward, the parents encourage their children to discuss the character's experiences, helping them connect the story to real-world situations and reinforcing the idea that understanding others can lead to positive relationships.

Empathy Exercises

Encourage parents to engage their children in empathy-building activities, such as volunteering, community service, or role-playing scenarios where they must consider different perspectives.

Example of a Real-Life Scenario: A child participates in a community service project, helping pack meals for needy families. Through this experience, they learn about the challenges others face and how small acts of kindness can make a big difference. The parents guide a discussion about how understanding and respecting the circumstances of others can lead to a more compassionate world.

Storytime and Role-Playing

Read age-appropriate books that depict characters from different backgrounds and experiences. After reading, you can engage in role-playing activities where children take on the perspectives of the characters.

Example of a Real-Life Scenario: After reading a story about a child who recently moved to a new country, parents guide their child to imagine how they might feel in a similar situation. This helps the child develop empathy and understanding for others facing similar challenges.

Cultural Celebrations and Traditions

You can involve your children in celebrating various cultural holidays, traditions, or festivals. This hands-on approach allows children to learn about different customs, foods, and practices, fostering an appreciation for diversity.

Example of a Real-Life Scenario: A family decides to celebrate a holiday from a different culture, such as Diwali or Hanukkah. They engage in activities related to the holiday, discuss its significance, and explore how different cultures commemorate special occasions.

Celebrating Hanukkah with your child can help them explore how different cultures celebrate holidays.
https://unsplash.com/photos/BsGQHOuOo0k?utm_source=unsplash&utm_medium=referral&utm_content=creditShareLink

Friendship and Pen Pal Exchanges

Encourage forming friendships with children from different backgrounds in person or through pen pal programs. These interactions help children build connections, exchange perspectives, and discover common ground.

Example of a Real-Life Scenario: Parents help their child connect with a pen pal from a different country. The child learns about their pen pal's daily life, hobbies, and interests by writing letters or emails, fostering cross-cultural understanding.

Art and Creativity

Have your children engage in art and creative projects that encourage them to express their understanding of diversity. Artistic activities like drawing, painting, or crafting can help children visually represent their thoughts and feelings about different cultures and perspectives.

Example of a Real-Life Scenario: Parents provide art supplies and ask their child to create a collage that represents the idea of "unity in diversity." The child selects images, colors, and symbols that illustrate their understanding of different cultures coming together.

Nature and Environmental Exploration

Take your children on nature walks or visits to botanical gardens, encouraging them to explore and appreciate the beauty of diverse plant and animal species. This experience can serve as a metaphor for valuing and respecting the uniqueness of individuals.

Example of a Real-Life Scenario: While on a nature walk, parents engage their children in a conversation about the different types of flowers they see and how each contributes to the overall beauty of the environment. They draw parallels between the diversity in nature and the diversity of people in the world.

Problem-Solving Games

Introduce your children to problem-solving games requiring collaboration and understanding differing viewpoints. Board games or activities involving group decisions can teach children the importance of listening and compromising.

Example of a Real-Life Scenario: Parents organize a family game night featuring a cooperative board game where players must work together to solve challenges. Through gameplay, children learn to consider diverse ideas and cooperate to achieve a common goal.

Cooking and Cultural Cuisine

You can involve children in cooking meals from different cultures, using this opportunity to discuss the traditions and histories associated with various dishes. This sensory experience helps children connect with different cultures on a personal level.

Example of a Real-Life Scenario: Parents and children prepare a traditional dish from another country, such as sushi or tacos. While cooking, the parents share information about the cultural significance of the meal and its role in the community.

Field Trips and Community Involvement

You can take your children on field trips to places of worship, community centers, or cultural events to expose them to different belief systems and lifestyles. Engaging with local communities helps children gain a broader perspective on the world around them.

Example of a Real-Life Scenario: A family visits a local cultural fair, where they interact with individuals from various backgrounds and discuss customs, traditions, and values.

Problem-Solving Scenarios

You can present your children with hypothetical scenarios involving conflicts or misunderstandings, encouraging them to brainstorm solutions that promote understanding and respect.

Example of a Real-Life Scenario: Parents describe a situation where two friends have different opinions about a game they want to play. The child suggests ways the friends could communicate, compromise, and find a solution that respects both viewpoints.

Encourage Curiosity and Questions

You should create an environment where children feel comfortable asking questions about differences. You need to address their inquiries with patience and provide age-appropriate explanations.

Example of a Real-Life Scenario: A child asks their parent why a classmate wears a headscarf. The parent explains that different people have different beliefs and practices, and respecting and understanding those differences is important.

Chapter 9: Bullying - Standing Up and Speaking Out

In this chapter, you will learn about the negative mental, emotional, and physical impact that bullying can have on children. You will know how to explain bullying and its different types to your child. You will also learn about the signs that indicate your child is a victim of bullying and learn several practical techniques, including role-play exercises and confidence-building strategies to help your child stand up for themselves.

Bullying in all its forms is harmful to children.
https://www.pexels.com/photo/a-sad-boy-sitting-on-a-floor-of-a-classroom-7929416/

Types of Bullying

People sometimes accidentally hurt each other and apologize when they realize what they have done. Bullying, on the other hand, is the act of hurting someone intentionally, over and over again. Bullies don't own up to their mistakes because they don't care about other people's feelings. Bullying can come in several forms: physical, verbal, social, and cyberbullying.

Physical Bullying

This includes pushing, tripping, punching, hitting, kicking, or pinching others. Bullies might also damage the belongings of their victims. Physical bullying is anything that hurts the victim's body or belongings.

Verbal Bullying

Verbal bullying is when the bully uses words to hurt others. They might insult, scare, intimidate, threaten, tease, or call them names. While verbal bullying might not lead to physical damage, it results in mental and emotional issues.

Social Bullying

Social bullying is the hardest type of bullying to recognize because it isn't always directly directed at the victim. Instead, it involves talking badly behind their back, spreading rumors about them, humiliating them, or ruining their reputation. Social bullies can also pull embarrassing pranks on their victims, mimic them harshly, give them unpleasant looks, make negative gestures, or encourage others not to talk to them.

Cyberbullying

Cyberbullying is done online. Victims may receive hurtful and insulting text messages or emails or inappropriate or mocking images, videos, or posts. They might be excluded from group chats and other online spaces. Bullies might spread rumors and gossip about the victim as well.

The Impact of Bullying on Overall Well-Being

Bullying can leave lasting mental and emotional scars, regardless of whether it occurred at home, sports practice, school, or online. It can interfere with the victim's ability to complete daily tasks.

Mental Health

Being a victim of bullying alters your child's sense of self and self-perception. This can negatively influence how they make decisions and handle other aspects of their lives, impacting their future mental, social, emotional, and professional health. Children who have been subject to any kind of bullying are more likely to seek professional mental health help in their adulthood.

Victims of bullying are at risk of developing anxiety and depression and experiencing persistent self-esteem issues. They usually feel lonely and unwanted and might even display sudden acts of violence.

In cases of severe bullying, the victim might resort to suicide to escape the mental, emotional, or physical torment. In other cases, bullying, alongside other sources of trauma, can lead to intense feelings of lack of belonging, hopelessness, and helplessness, which might lead to suicidal thoughts or tendencies.

If your child is struggling, they might avoid school and other places where they might meet their bullies. This can result in a decline in their academic performance and social well-being.

Self-Esteem

Being bullied can make your child feel insecure and tense all the time. They never know when their bully is going to pull their next move, making them feel on edge. Feeling unaccepted and excluded from their community can cause your child to withdraw further and experience constant feelings of anger and frustration. They might also constantly search for ways in which they won't attract any attention to themselves. This might cause them to miss out on opportunities to have fun, make friends, and learn new things.

Physical Health

Aside from the visible effects of physical bullying, all types of bullying can have a negative impact on your child's physical well-being. They might have little or no appetite at all, trouble regulating their breathing and heart rate, and sleep issues like insomnia or oversleeping. Being constantly on edge, stressed, and anxious can also result in detrimental health problems.

Telltale Signs Your Child Is Being Bullied

Loss of Interest in Activities

Your child is likely being bullied if you notice that they have suddenly lost interest in activities they once enjoyed. For instance, if they enjoyed partaking in their school's sports team or after-school clubs but suddenly withdrew from them, they could be teased or harassed.

Changes in Sleeping or Eating Habits

Stress results in changes in a child's eating and sleeping habits. If they're eating less than usual, this might indicate a loss of appetite due to overthinking. If they're eating more than usual, they might be experiencing emotional eating, or it could be because their lunch is being taken at school. Changes in eating habits can also indicate that they're being teased for their appearance or weight. They might have trouble falling or staying asleep due to overthinking, anxiety, or nightmares.

Increased Irritability

Your child might become very moody and irritable if they're victims of bullying. The tension, worry, fear, and sorrow that come with abuse can leave them feeling frustrated or short-tempered, especially before they leave for school or after they come back.

Faking Sickness

If your child often uses stomachaches, headaches, or other physical symptoms to avoid going to school (or get out of it early), they might be trying to avoid bullies. Make sure to rule out health conditions first.

Academic Decline

Focusing on their homework, projects, tests, and studies can be the least of your child's worries if they're being tormented in school. If they're putting in less effort in school and getting worse grades than usual, they might feel pressured by their abusers.

Fidgeting

If your child is naturally calm and collected but has recently started fidgeting, it might be because they're being bullied. Fidgeting is a sign of the fight or flight response triggered by stressful and frightening situations. This response leads to being hyper-aware of one's environment so you can flee or take action whenever danger is imminent.

Avoiding Talking about School

If your child avoids answering questions about their day or school in general, this might be another sign that they're a victim of bullying. They might be embarrassed about the fact that they're getting bullied and wish to hide it.

Taking It Out Elsewhere

Your child might be bullied if they're showing sudden aggressive and violent tendencies. They naturally feel the need to take out their anger and frustration somewhere else. They might even start picking on their siblings or other children. They might mimic what is going on with them because they don't know how else to deal with their anger. Other sudden personality changes should also be reasons for concern.

Injuries and Bruises

Unexplained injuries and bruises are among the most obvious telltale signs that your child is being physically bullied. You might also notice that their belongings frequently get damaged or missing. Your child might make up stories for their wounds and damaged items because they're scared or ashamed to tell you about the bullying. They might also fear their bully will get back at them for telling.

These are only a few potential signs that your child is being bullied. You know your child more than anyone, so make sure to consider any changes in their behaviors and actions. Be patient with them and let them know that you have their back and that you'll work on finding a solution together.

Strategies to Deal with Bullying

Role-Play Scenarios

You should try role-playing bullying scenarios with your child to teach them how to effectively respond to the harassment.

• Scenario 1 (Verbal Bullying)

The aim of this first scenario is to demonstrate to your child how to act in these situations. You will role-play as your child, and your child will act as the bully.

Bully: You look horrible today! What kind of outfit is this? Everyone hates it!

Child: *Thank you for your opinion. I really like my outfit today, though.*

The child should be calm and collected while responding to the bully.

• Scenario 2 (Verbal Bullying)

Now that you've demonstrated how your child should respond to verbal bullying, it's your turn to role-play as the bully and have them respond.

Bully: Look at *your child's name,* the nerd!

If your child needs help responding calmly, you can help them find the right words. Ideally, the response should be something along these lines:

I enjoy reading and learning about different things! I don't mind you calling me a nerd.

The main goal here is to teach your child to respond confidently and calmly to bullying. They should show the bully that they're not affected by their words and that they're proud of their choices, interests, and tastes.

- **Scenario 3 (Cyberbullying)**

Use this scenario to demonstrate how your child should respond to cyberbullying. You get to role-play as your child, and your child acts as the bully.

Bully: (Commenting on your child's picture) You look funny in this picture! Your forehead looks huge, hahaha.

Child: *That's not nice! I think I look great here; that's why I posted it. I'm going to report your comment for being hurtful.*

Your child should report the comment and block the bully.

- **Scenario 4 (Cyberbullying)**

It's your turn to role-play as the bully.

Bully: (In the group chat) Did you know that *your child's name* failed all the tests? What a loser!

Any action that shows that your child is calm and unaffected is right. For instance, they can say the following.

Child: *That's not true. I didn't fail my tests. Why don't we all focus on true and positive things to discuss instead?*

Encourage your child to incorporate what they learned into the following 2 scenarios.

- **Scenario 5 (Physical Bullying)**

Bully: (pushes your child)

An ideal response would be:

Child: *I don't like being pushed. What makes you think it's okay to treat others this way? (leaves)*

- **Scenario 6 (Standing Up for Victims of Bullying)**

Bully: (mocks your child's friend)

Your child should calmly approach the bully and let them know that their actions are unacceptable.

Child: *Hey! It's not okay to treat others like that! Let's be kind to each other.*

Help Your Child Build Their Confidence

- Teach them the importance of positive affirmations and how to use them. Together with your child, create a list of positive affirmations about them and remind them to repeat them daily. This will improve their confidence and self-esteem.
- Celebrate even their smallest achievements together and remind them of how proud you are of them.
- Buy them a nice-looking journal and encourage them to use it every day.
- Support your child's hobbies and interests. If they like art, for instance, sign them up for a painting class.
- Enroll your child in non-school-related extracurricular activities, such as music, dance, or sports classes.
- Teach them mindfulness and relaxation techniques, such as breathwork and meditation. This will boost their self-awareness and help them effectively deal with difficult situations.

Teach Them to Report Bullying Incidents to Trusted Adults

Teaching your child to report bullying incidents is crucial for their safety and the well-being of other victims. Encouraging your child to speak up against bullies teaches them that reaching out for help is not a sign of weakness and is a positive step toward healthy conflict resolution. Reporting to trusted adults ensures that the situation is dealt with. This way, no other children fall victim to the bully's harmful ways. It also teaches your child how to communicate their thoughts and feelings and sets an example for others to report incidents.

Bullying can affect several aspects of your child's life and leave lasting emotional and mental scars. Recognizing signs that your child is being bullied will allow you to step in when needed. You should also teach them how to respond assertively and confidently to their bullies. Encouraging them to report bullying incidents to trusted adults, working on improving their confidence, and keeping open communication are all steps in the right direction.

Chapter 10: Ten Techniques to Cultivate Harmonious Relationships and Social Skills in Children

In this chapter, you will learn about the role of healthy and secure relationships and great communication skills in your child's growth and development. You will find the 10 techniques you need to incorporate into your interactions with them to teach them the social skills they need the most. Finally, you'll find examples of scenarios you can use to showcase these techniques to your child.

The Importance of Social Skills and Healthy Relationships

Healthy and Secure Relationships

Building healthy relationships is crucial for your child's mental, emotional, and social development. Secure relationships teach children to manage their actions and emotions and allow them to develop empathy. The relationships that children form with their friends, family, teachers, and caregivers shape the way they learn about themselves and the world around them.

Relationships offer a space in which children can express their thoughts and feelings. They offer something, such as a glimpse into their emotions or a question, and wait to receive empathy or an answer in return. What they receive from others translates into information regarding communication and acceptable social behavior. It helps them understand how they should think, behave, and communicate with others and gives them insight into the level at which they should show a sense of understanding or express their emotions.

Relationships offer a space in which children can express their thoughts and feelings.
https://www.pexels.com/photo/toddlers-forming-a-circle-754769/

The relationships your child builds at an early age set the tone for what they will expect from others in a relationship and how they'll treat them in the future. This is why cultivating harmonious and secure relationships is essential for your child's healthy growth and development.

Social Skills

1. Relationship-Building

Good social skills equip your child with all the tools they need to build healthy relationships with others: effective communication, active listening, conflict resolution, and empathy. Social skills allow people to express themselves in friendly yet assertive and clear ways. It allows them to respect other people's beliefs and perspectives even when they're different from their own. People with good social skills can find solutions that satisfy all parties involved to prevent the problem from escalating further.

2. Self-Confidence

Self-confidence leads to a positive relationship with others and with oneself. Having positive self-perception allows people to express themselves assertively and set healthy boundaries in their relationships with others. Good self-esteem will allow your child to easily manage awkward situations, quickly recover from rejection or failure, and pursue their goals, hobbies, and passions.

3. Better Communication

You can only go so far without effective communication skills. These skills are the key to thriving in relationships, academic endeavors, and the workplace. Great communication skills allow individuals to securely position themselves in their community and workplaces. They can avoid and deal with misunderstandings and potential conflicts by incorporating their problem-solving strategies, empathy, and active listening skills into their interactions.

4. Empathy and Understanding

Good social skills allow children to respect and appreciate differences between people. They ensure that children acknowledge and understand various viewpoints, avoid judging others, and relate to them. Empathy is an important social skill that helps children express their compassion for people and approach them with kindness and respect.

10 Techniques to Incorporate into Your Daily Interactions

1. Active Listening

There is no better way to teach your child this technique than by modeling it yourself. Active listening skills allow others to feel heard and give them the impression that you really care about them. It shows others that their words, stories, and experiences matter, which fosters mutual openness and trust. Active listening requires paying full attention to the speaker, understanding and reflecting on their words, responding mindfully and thoughtfully, avoiding interrupting them, and maintaining adequate eye contact throughout the interaction.

Example: Your child returns from school excited to tell you about their day. Even if you're busy, take 10 minutes of your time to listen to what they have to say. Show that you're interested, ask them questions, face them, maintain eye contact, and respond with the same level of enthusiasm. This will not only model the type of behavior they need to display in their interactions, but it will also strengthen your bond with your child and show them that their feelings and experiences matter.

2. Empathy

Empathy leads to more fruitful and fulfilling relationships, as it helps you understand people's thoughts and feelings on a deeper level. It makes it easier to communicate with others and be supportive when they need you. To help your child cultivate empathy, encourage them to examine situations from various perspectives. For instance, if they got into an argument with their friend, ask them to think about how their friend felt in that situation. This will help them relate to how others feel. Being empathetic toward them will validate their emotions, help them feel understood, and encourage them to do the same with others.

Example: Your child is upset because their plans with their friends got canceled. Instead of ignoring them or showing frustration because of their complaining, tell them you understand how they feel. You can say that you know they're disappointed because their plans didn't follow through, but sometimes things don't go as planned. Validating their emotions can help them build empathy over time.

3. Sharing and Cooperation

Engage in activities that encourage your child to cooperate and share things. You can do arts and crafts, play board games, or play video games together. Doing things together is a great opportunity to spend quality time with your child while teaching them the importance of compromise and helping them develop teamwork and cooperation skills.

Example: Organize weekly game nights with your family. Get together to play board or card games or to solve problems together. As you play, work together to develop strategies and helpful ideas. Make sure to encourage each other even if you are playing on different teams. Your child will develop good sportsmanship, understand the importance of teamwork, and learn about compromise and how everyone can work towards a common goal while using different strategies.

4. Conflict Resolution

Approaching conflicts calmly and being open to discussing them along with various solutions will allow children to learn conflict resolution skills. Encourage your child to express their feelings, share their viewpoint, and listen to the perspectives of others before they rush to make a decision or say something they might regret later.

Example: If your children are fighting over a toy, guide them toward resolving the conflict independently. Ask them to think of solutions that will make everyone happy. Doing this every time a disagreement arises will train them to communicate effectively and think of satisfactory solutions.

5. Politeness

Teach your children about the importance of being polite and maintaining good manners. Say "thank you," "please," and similar courteous expressions even when you're talking to them to model this behavior. Explain that being polite shows respect and gratitude to others – essential to building and maintaining healthy relationships.

6. Effective Communication

Teach your children that effective communication differs from one situation and context to the other. For instance, how they speak to friends differs from how they speak to adult family members, teachers, and strangers. Teach them how appropriate personal space also depends on the context.

Example: Have your child listen to how you communicate during a work-related phone call versus how you interact with your friends. Reflect on the changes in your tone and choice of words with your child. You can also role-play scenarios with them in which you ask them to demonstrate how they would describe their favorite movie to a friend and then their teacher.

7. Body Language and Non-Verbal Cues

70% to 93% of all human communications are non-verbal. Non-verbal means of communication are often more honest and insightful than verbal ones. Hand gestures, facial expressions, posture, and body language can help you understand how others feel, enriching your interactions. Teaching your child the impact of non-verbal cues and how to observe, interpret, and apply them will boost their communication and social skills.

Example: If you're watching a movie together, pause every time a character visibly expresses their emotions and ask your child how they think they feel. Ask them to analyze the hand gestures, facial expressions, and body language used to be as accurate as possible.

8. Kindness and Positivity

Kindness and positivity are two great qualities to have in a friend. Discuss with your child how being kind, positive, and supportive can help them build lasting, healthy friendships with others. Ask them to think about the qualities they believe make a good friend and guide them towards modeling these behaviors by portraying them yourself.

Example: You can bake cookies with your child on a rainy day to share them with your neighbors. Habitually think of ways in which you can make someone's day better without expecting anything in return.

9. Dealing with Rejection

Your child is bound to encounter rejection at some point in life. Not everyone will want to be their friend or reciprocate their kindness or support. Teach them that rejection is not a reflection of who they are as a person. Teach them that rejection shouldn't affect their self-esteem and confidence.

Example: Imagine that your child didn't get cast as the lead in a play they were excited about. Instead of telling them to get over it, you should validate their emotions and reassure them that it doesn't mean they're not good enough. Tell them that it's okay to be upset, but they shouldn't let this situation define them. Remind them to be proud of their efforts and that more opportunities will come in the future.

10. Cultural Sensitivity

Expose your child to different viewpoints and backgrounds through movies, books, or travel. Educate them about the importance of respecting and learning about different cultures and their customs, celebrations, and traditions. Teaching your child to accept and appreciate the differences between people can set them up for professional and interpersonal success in the future.

How to Teach Your Child These Techniques

- Model these behaviors as children are visual and observant learners. They also often copy their parents, which is why you must only show them the behaviors you want them to adopt.

- Come up with role-playing scenarios that allow your child to put each of the aforementioned techniques to use. Switch roles to teach them about different perspectives.

- Dedicate 10 minutes before their bedtime toward reflection. Encourage them to share their experiences with you and talk to you about any challenges they faced, the emotions they experienced, how they wanted to react, and what they did instead. Discuss ways in which they can swiftly handle similar situations in the future.

- Watch and read age-appropriate and educational books, movies, and TV shows to observe and interpret the social skills and behaviors portrayed.

- Use rewards and compliments to reinforce good behavior and positive use of social skills.

- Maintain open communication channels with your child. Reassure them that they can share their thoughts, feelings, and experiences without being judged. Provide them with the support and guidance they need to thrive.

The behavior you model to your child will impact the way they treat others.
https://www.pexels.com/photo/students-running-together-inside-the-school-8926648/

Keep in mind that the behaviors you model to your child and all your interactions with them have a profound impact on the way they deal with others. This is not to scare you but to remind you that you have the power to teach your child invaluable techniques that will help them cultivate strong and fruitful bonds with others. Now that you've read this chapter, you understand how to encourage your child to approach others with confidence, empathy, and a sense of understanding.

Conclusion

As you turn the last page of this book, think about all the things your child has learned about conflict resolution, a skill that is not only useful but absolutely essential in every aspect of their lives. From standing up against bullies to finding solutions with friends and classmates, conflict resolution empowers children to navigate the world's complexities with confidence and grace. The lessons you've explored serve as the foundation for a lifetime of success, building strong leaders who can overcome challenges and make a positive impact.

Conflict is inevitable. When you arm your child with the tools and strategies this book presents, they can transform conflicts from stumbling blocks into stepping stones. This book has shown you that conflict resolution is not just about solving disagreements; it's about fostering understanding, empathy, and communication. It equips young minds with the ability to turn conflicts into opportunities for growth and connection.

Think about the countless situations where your child can benefit from these skills. Picture them confidently addressing a teacher who might be treating them unfairly or skillfully navigating a disagreement with a friend. Think of them stepping up as a mediator among classmates, finding common ground, and building bridges. These experiences aren't just about resolving conflicts – they are the building blocks of leadership. By learning to effectively manage conflicts, children develop the confidence to lead, inspire, and positively impact those around them.

You need to recognize that conflicts are an integral part of life. They exist everywhere your child goes, whether at school, home, or in the community. Avoiding conflicts might seem tempting, but in doing so, you miss out on valuable opportunities for growth and learning.

As a parent, you play a vital role in nurturing your child's conflict-resolution skills. Guide them through the lessons they've learned from this book and encourage them to incorporate them into their everyday lives. Ask them to maintain a conflict resolution journal – a safe space where they can reflect on their experiences, jot down their feelings, and explore potential solutions. When they encounter conflicts, ask them to look at their journal and consider how they can apply their knowledge to overcome the challenge.

Practice makes perfect, and role-playing conflict scenarios can be an invaluable tool. Act out different situations with your child, allowing them to practice their conflict resolution skills in a supportive environment. The more they engage in these scenarios, the more confident they will become in using their newfound abilities when real-life conflicts arise. Remember, instilling confidence in your child is key. Remind them of their strengths, acknowledge their progress, and celebrate their successes – no matter how small.

Check out another book in the series

References

(N.d.). Eccpct.com. https://www.eccpct.com/Resources/Child/Tips-for-Tots/Help-Young-Children-with-Conflict-Resolution/

5 Strategies to help your Child with Autism Spectrum Disorder develop Social Skills. (2019, March 8). Brainfit Kids. https://brainfitkids.net.au/2019/03/5-strategies-to-help-your-child-with-autism-spectrum-disorder-develop-social-skills/

5 Ways to Boost Your Child's Confidence. (n.d.). On Our Sleeves. https://www.onoursleeves.org/mental-wellness-tools-guides/healthy-habits/boost-kids-confidence

7 key strategies to manage sibling rivalry. (n.d.). Big Life Journal. https://biglifejournal.com/blogs/blog/key-strategies-manage-sibling-rivalry

Active listening. (2023, January 23). Cdc.gov. https://www.cdc.gov/parents/essentials/toddlersandpreschoolers/communication/activelistening.html

Admin, W. (2023). How do you teach children cultural awareness and diversity? Mindful and Modern ABA Therapies. https://montessoriaba.com/teach-children-cultural-awareness-diversityhow-do-you-teach-children-cultural-awareness-and-diversity/

Amy Morin, L. (2018, February 7). 6 parenting strategies for raising emotionally intelligent kids. Verywell Family. https://www.verywellfamily.com/tips-for-raising-an-emotionally-intelligent-child-4157946

Arias, J. (2020, April 8). Activities to help children recognize and explain their emotions. BSN Voices; The British School in The Netherlands. https://voices.britishschool.nl/2020/04/08/activities-to-help-children-recognise-and-explain-their-emotions/

Ayvazo, S., Brill, A., & Magal, K. S. (2023). The Problem Solver: A behavioral intervention for teaching problem solving to high-functioning students with autism. Teaching Exceptional Children, 55(3), 208–219. https://doi.org/10.1177/00400599211068444

Clara. (2022, May 8). 20 Fun Conflict Resolution Activities for Kids (printable PDF): Worksheets, games, and activities. Very Special Tales. https://veryspecialtales.com/conflict-resolution-activities-for-kids-pdf/

Clara. (2023, January 30). 28 fun, emotional Intelligence Activities for kids. Very Special Tales. https://veryspecialtales.com/emotional-intelligence-activities-for-kids/

Core values for conflict management. (n.d.). Conflict Management at Iowa - The University of Iowa. https://conflictmanagement.org.uiowa.edu/core-values-conflict-management

Croghan, M., & Mann, M. (n.d.). 5 ways to help kids become collaborative problem-solvers. Nesta. https://www.nesta.org.uk/blog/5-ways-to-help-kids-become-collaborative-problem-solvers/

Department of Health & Human Services. (n.d.). Young children and communication. Better Health Channel. https://www.betterhealth.vic.gov.au/health/healthyliving/young-children-and-communication#communicating-with-an-older-child

Education, V. (2022, February 11). Why Social Skills are Important for Child Development. Vanco. https://www.vancopayments.com/education/blog/social-skills-in-child-development

Empathy: The Key to Deepening Relationships | Blog | Marshall Connects | Ontario, Canada. (2017, July 29). https://www.marshallconnects.com/site/corporate-growth-news/2017/07/29/how-empathy-can-enhance-your-relationships

Engler, B. (2022, September 2). Teaching your child to deal with conflict – connections academy®. Connectionsacademy.com; Connections Academy. https://www.connectionsacademy.com/support/resources/article/building-conflict-resolution-skills-in-children/

Engler, B. (2023). Teaching Your Child to Deal with Conflict. www.connectionsacademy.com. https://www.connectionsacademy.com/support/resources/article/building-conflict-resolution-skills-in-children/

Garey, J., Lee, S. A., & Werley, C. (2020, August 26). Teaching kids how to deal with conflict. Child Mind Institute. https://childmind.org/article/teaching-kids-how-to-deal-with-conflict/

Hadani, H. S., & Katz, R. (2022, June 22). Talking about emotions: How to support children's social and emotional development through language. Brookings. https://www.brookings.edu/articles/talking-about-emotions-how-to-support-childrens-social-and-emotional-development-through-language/

Helping kids handle conflict. (2018, July 13). Kids Helpline. https://kidshelpline.com.au/parents/issues/helping-kids-handle-conflict

Helping kids handle conflict. (2018, July 13). Kids Helpline. https://kidshelpline.com.au/parents/issues/helping-kids-handle-conflict

Holt, K. (2023). 10 Ways to Stop & Prevent Bullying at School. Mom Loves Best. https://momlovesbest.com/bullying-prevention

How does bullying affect your child? | Family Lives. (n.d.). https://www.familylives.org.uk/advice/bullying/advice-for-parents/how-does-bullying-affect-your-child

How to share a negotiation education with kids. (2022, August 11). PON - Program on Negotiation at Harvard Law School; Program on Negotiation at Harvard Law School. https://www.pon.harvard.edu/daily/leadership-skills-daily/teaching-children-to-self-advocate-nb/

How to teach preschoolers about conflict resolution. (2021, January 25). The Pillars Christian Learning Centers; The Pillars Christian Learning Center. https://thepillarsclc.com/conflict-resolution-for-preschoolers/

Howley-Rouse, A. (2020, March 25). Supporting children's emotional learning in early childhood. THE EDUCATION HUB. https://theeducationhub.org.nz/supporting-childrens-emotional-learning-in-early-childhood/

Improve your child's active listening skills. (2017, June 13). Oxford Learning. https://www.oxfordlearning.com/improve-active-listening-skills/

It, O. (2019, February 18). 6 fun games to teach active listening. KITS - Kids In Transition To School. https://kidsintransitiontoschool.org/6-fun-games-to-teach-active-listening/

Jarocha, T. (2023). 12 Tips for Raising Confident Kids. Child Mind Institute. https://childmind.org/article/12-tips-raising-confident-kids/

Lora, C. C., Kisamore, A. N., Reeve, K. F., & Townsend, D. B. (2019). Effects of a problem-solving strategy on the independent completion of vocational tasks by adolescents with autism spectrum disorder. Journal of Applied Behavior Analysis, jaba.558. https://doi.org/10.1002/jaba.558

MasterClass. (2021, November 2). How to Use Active Listening to Improve Your Communication Skills - 2023 - MasterClass. https://www.masterclass.com/articles/how-to-use-active-listening-to-improve-your-communication-skills

Merrow, C. (2021, June 15). Active listening skills for kids. Empowering Education. https://empoweringeducation.org/blog/active-listening/

Mission, values, and beliefs, & strategic governance. (n.d.). Teaching emotional intelligence in early childhood. NAEYC. https://www.naeyc.org/resources/pubs/yc/mar2017/teaching-emotional-intelligence

Moonpreneur. (2023, March 3). Why are social skills important for Kids? Moonpreneur. https://moonpreneur.com/blog/social-skills-important-for-kids/

No title. (n.d.). Com.Pk. https://www.twinkl.com.pk/teaching-wiki/active-listening

No title. (n.d.). Com.Pk. https://www.twinkl.com.pk/resource/us-t2-p-268-compromises-activity

No title. (n.d.). Whatdoesmammasay.com. https://whatdoesmammasay.com/cgi-sys/suspendedpage.cgi

Peterson, S. (2016, June 29). Tolerance. Beyond Intractability. https://www.beyondintractability.org/essay/tolerance

Pin on emotions/parenting. (n.d.). Pinterest. https://www.pinterest.co.uk/pin/682787993501459793/feedback/?invite_code=aa25ba6883124fefb86740206cc8f497&sender_id=682788130914495615

Psych, B. D. (2020). The Effects of Bullying on Mental Health. Best Day Psychiatry & Counseling. https://bestdaypsych.com/the-effects-of-bullying-on-mental-health/

Related Links Discussion Questions. (n.d.). Related KidsHealth Links. Kidshealth.org. https://classroom.kidshealth.org/classroom/3to5/personal/growing/conflict_resolution.pdf

Relationships and child development. (2023, March 22). Raising Children Network. https://raisingchildren.net.au/newborns/development/understanding-development/relationships-development

Sanford Health News. (2021, July 7). Raise a polite kid: Everyone appreciates good manners. Sanford Health News. https://news.sanfordhealth.org/parenting/everyone-appreciates-good-manners/

Scaife, A. (2017, February 15). Negotiation and the art of compromise. Family Times.

Segal, J., Robinson, L., & Melinda Smith, M. A. (n.d.). Conflict resolution skills - Helpguide.org. https://www.helpguide.org/articles/relationships-communication/conflict-resolution-skills.htm

Sichterman, J. (2015, December 9). Teaching your Child, the Art of Negotiation. Embracing Horizons. https://embracinghorizons.com/teaching-your-child-the-art-of-negotiation/

Suarez, V. D., Najdowski, A. C., Tarbox, J., Moon, E., St. Clair, M., & Farag, P. (2022). Teaching individuals with autism problem-solving skills for resolving social conflicts. Behavior Analysis in Practice, 15(3), 768–781. https://doi.org/10.1007/s40617-021-00643-y

Teach emotional intelligence to children with these 30 powerful activities. (2020, November 8). Bettering Youth; Bettering Youth: Tutoring. https://betteringyouth.co.uk/blog/emotional-literacy-30-activities

Teach emotional intelligence to children with these 30 powerful activities. (2020, November 8). Bettering Youth; Bettering Youth: Tutoring. https://betteringyouth.co.uk/blog/emotional-literacy-30-activities

Teaching conflict resolution skills for kids: A parent's guide. (2023, June 30). BrightChamps Blog; BrightChamps. https://brightchamps.com/blog/conflict-resolution-skills-for-kids/

Teaching kids to negotiate. (2002, September 25). FamilyEducation. https://www.familyeducation.com/kids/development/emotional/teaching-kids-negotiate

Translations, S. (2020, October 8). The role of language in emotions - Stillman Translations. Stillman Translations. https://www.stillmantranslations.com/role-of-language-emotions/

Tutt, P. (2021, August 5). 7 ways to teach kids to manage their own conflicts. Edutopia; George Lucas Educational Foundation. https://www.edutopia.org/article/7-ways-teach-kids-manage-their-own-conflicts/

Types Of Bullying | National Centre Against Bullying. (n.d.). https://www.ncab.org.au/bullying-advice/bullying-for-parents/types-of-bullying/

Understanding and managing emotions: children and teenagers. (2022, October 18). Raising Children Network. https://raisingchildren.net.au/preschoolers/development/preschoolers-social-emotional-development/understanding-managing-emotions-children-teenagers

Using emotional language: How to talk to your kids about feelings. (n.d.). Nationwidechildrens.org. https://www.nationwidechildrens.org/family-resources-education/700childrens/2019/01/using-emotional-language

Valente, S., Afonso Lourenço, A., & Németh, Z. (2022). School conflicts: Causes and management strategies in classroom relationships. In M. P. Levine (Ed.), Interpersonal Relationships. IntechOpen.

Warger, C. (2018, July 30). Why students with autism spectrum disorder have difficulty with math word problem-solving. Exceptional Innovations. https://www.exinn.net/autism-math-word-problem-solving/

Why relationships are so important for children and young people. (n.d.). Mental Health Foundation. https://www.mentalhealth.org.uk/explore-mental-health/blogs/why-relationships-are-so-important-children-and-young-people

Yetty. (2022). 10 Telltale Signs Your Child is Being Bullied. LagosMums. https://lagosmums.com/10-telltale-signs-your-child-is-being-bullied/

Young, K. (2020). 5 Ways to Prepare Your Child to Deal With Rejection. Hey Sigmund. https://www.heysigmund.com/5-ways-to-prepare-your-child-for-rejection/

Zurn, M. (n.d.). Learning to Share and Cooperate Leads to Friendship - Primrose Schools. Primrose Schools. https://www.primroseschools.com/blog/learning-to-share-and-cooperate-leads-to-friendship-2

Printed in Great Britain
by Amazon

44537141R00059